Confluences 3

Essays on the New Canadian Literature

edited by

Dannabang Kuwabong

MAWENZI
HOUSE

We acknowledge the support of the Canada Council for the Arts for our publishing program. We also acknowledge support from the Government of Ontario through the Ontario Arts Council, and the support of the Government of Canada through the Canada Book Fund.

ONTARIO ARTS COUNCIL
CONSEIL DES ARTS DE L'ONTARIO
an Ontario government agency
un organisme du gouvernement de l'Ontario

Canada Council for the Arts Conseil des arts du Canada

Canada

Cover photo: scol22 / Geese at Sunrise stock photo / istockphoto.com

Library and Archives Canada Cataloguing in Publication

Title: Confluences 3 : essays on the new Canadian literature / edited by Dannabang Kuwabong.

Other titles: Confluences three

Names: Kuwabong, Dannabang, 1955- editor.

Description: Includes bibliographical references.

Identifiers: Canadiana (print) 20210317442 | Canadiana (ebook) 20210317450 | ISBN 9781774150474 (softcover) | ISBN 9781774150481 (EPUB) | ISBN 9781774150498 (PDF)

Subjects: LCSH: Canadian literature—20th century—History and criticism. | LCSH: Canadian literature—21st century—History and criticism. | LCGFT: Essays.

Classification: LCC PS8117 .C663 2021 | DDC C810.9/0054—dc23

Printed and bound in Canada by Coach House Printing.

Mawenzi House Publishers Ltd.
39 Woburn Avenue (B)
Toronto, Ontario M5M 1K5
Canada
www.mawenzihouse.com

Contents

Preface

Confluences 3: Essays on the New Canadian Literature follows the pioneering work of Nurjehan Aziz and MG Vassanji, with Mawenzi House Publishers, to foster greater critical awareness of some of the finest new writers in Canada, whose work—with a few exceptions—because of critical racism have yet to receive significant acceptance and appraisal. When noticed, the work is summarily dismissed as "ethnic" or "multicultural" and hence not Canadian enough. Claire Harris's 1994 statement encodes this succinctly: "Needless to say (but I am going to say it), this is not a subject which either my adopted country, Canada, or the larger Western culture can accept with equanimity. Thus marginalization by literary category: Immigrant Literature/Writing by Women of Colour/Feminist Writing/Political Literature/Post Colonial Literature/New Literature in English" (28). To George Elliott Clarke, these categorizations are designed as critical play games of delay or denial of the importance of non-Euro-Canadian writers to the growth of Canadian literature. These categories are the batons of the critical and literary gendarmeries, who guard the hierarchical and patriarchal structures of Canadian literary culture. Thus, with *Confluences 1, 2, 3*, Mawenzi House lays claim to the category of "New Literature" as a strategy of critical and literary empowerment. In so doing, these volumes establish place of refuge, growth, and recognition for these writers. This series is a step forward in generating greater interest in the study of these marginalized authors by scholars interested in them, and not waiting for mainstream scholars to one day see them.

Yet it is true that occasionally Canadian literary journals issue special editions that focus on the work of a few well-known "minority" writers. However, there is no sustained program of inclusion of these writers for study in the Canadian canon. The excuses: we do not understand their work; they write about other places; their language is too eclectic or idiosyncratic. The tokenish and dismissive manner in which these new voices are treated inspired the *Confluences* series of studies. *Confluences 1* was issued in 2016 with eleven essays and was shortly followed by *Confluences II* in 2017 with eight essays. This volume, *Confluences 3*, follows the trail. It includes excellent scholarly essays on poetry, fiction, and drama by writers, some of whom have received some measure of critical acclaim and others whose work so far is yet to be known.

"Pamela Mordecai and Canadian Literary Transcultural Eschatology," begins with a quote by Harold Bloom to assert that Pamela Mordecai's work "transumes every extra poetic belief" in contemporary Canadian Christian poetry (Bloom 96). The essay combs through Mordacai's work to reveal that the author engages her Jamaican creole language and creole identificatory cultural and literary maneuvers to challenge the dualistic and often racialized interpretations and practices of the Christian faith. This, she claims, will yield a fresher recasting of the New Testament that uses her Jamaican cultural, historical, linguistic, and performative roots for global plural cultural audiences. Mordecai's claim to relevance then as a Canadian author rises from her originality, which sets her apart. Her originality also stems from her refusal to be consumed with the issues of multiculturalism and racism that are often used to read non-Euro-Canadian texts. Furthermore, the essay argues, Mordecai joins an exclusive club of Canadian poets who celebrate their Christian faith without apologies. Mordecai's work endeavors to break down literary. linguistic, and spiritual boundaries in Canada and in the process reenergizes Canadian literature.

Hugh Hazelton in "Other Languages in National Literatures: W H Hudson's English Argentina and Pablo Urbanyi's Argentine Canada," draws attention to an area of Canadian literature that has hardly been explored. For far too long Canadian literary studies have never considered the presence of Latin American writers in the Canadian landscape. Their almost total exclusion is not because they do not exist, but because the use of Spanish by Hudson and Urbanyi apparently disqualifies them. Hazleton begins by establishing the fallacy of using linguistic and geophysical homogeneity as the yardsticks for the construction of a national literature. He contends that in reality every so-called national literature has erupted from plural linguistic, literary, and cultural traditions. In the Americas, linguistic dynamism and cultural creolization has created a more democratic literary space that spotlights writers of other languages and origins. Hudson, a novelist, short-story writer, and naturalist was born of American parents and raised in Argentina in the mid-nineteenth century. He is an icon of Argentine culture even though he wrote exclusively in English. Hazleton compares Hudson's reception in Argentina with that of Pablo Urbanyi, a Hungarian-born Argentinian, in Canadian. Urbanyi is an important member of the Hispanic literary presence in Canada and treats predominantly Canadian themes, yet, though he is translated into English and French, his work is hardly mentioned in Canadian studies. Hazleton's essay sets out to provide provisional answers to this conundrum.

If the first two essays explore linguistic challenges to the Canadian canon, Leslie Sanders's "Racial Re/Profiling: the plays of Andrew Moodie" treats us to an intertextual reading of Andrew Moodie's drama and theatre, tracing and evaluating his work as a playwright, theatre director, actor, critic from 1995 to 2009. Moodie's plays, argues Sanders, seek to a centrl place for Blacks in Canada. His work revokes the explosion of imagined blackness in Black expressive, performance, and visual arts and reveals the lie in the image of the African Canadian as mired in misery, poverty, and victimhood. A journey with Moodie through his plays is a journey to an alternate reality in which African Canadians thrive, as opposed to the imagined world propagated by the dominant culture. The Canadian ideal of success can also be imagined, realized, enacted, and lived through Black bodies, even if in the process they still have to transgress injustice and racism.

Horace Goddard's essay introduces a poetic voice totally at odds with all that is theorized as African Canadian poetry. Goddard argues that to read Kuwabong is to be engaged in a three-faceted world: Ghana, the

Caribbean, and Canada. While African diaspora poets often construct their historical and cultural identities by going back to imagined or real African roots, Kuwabong reverses these journeys of identity formation. Goddard argues that perhaps this poet's odyssey is not actually a reversal, but a going forward to return. His rootedness in his Ghanaian homeplace enables him to conduct journeys through the Caribbean as pilgrimages of self-discovery and expansion; by discovering and acknowledging his Ghanaian roots, which were scattered in the trans-Atlantic slave trade, he is on the path to completion.

Kate Siklosi engages narrative hauntology as a reading paradigm of to enter into the liminal spaces projected in Marlene Nourbese Philip's *The Book of Un with Undex* (2017). Siklosi creates a discursive space that brings Philip's 2017 work to dialogue with her 2008 work Zong! and her 1989 highly praised yet understudied *She Tries Her Tongue, Her Silence Softly Breaks*. The need for this inter-text conversation is to explicate, Siklosi says, the limbo poetics of the ghosts of memories, a type of liminal knowledge that inform Philp's work. Siklosi sees Philip's sustained poetics of "Un" as knowledge-seeking and construction of hidden events from the past to the present that can be birthed through narrative hauntology. Haunting narratives are Philip's acts of uprising the ghosts of history that have lain unspoken and undermined by language manipulation.

Juan M Salomé Villarini draws attention to Shani Mootoo's narrative preoccupation with patriarchy, toxic masculinity, and gender-based violence in domestic spaces. His central argument involves the showcasing of violence, or what he calls "monstrous masculinity," which seems to have become the stereotypical label slapped on Indo-Caribbean men. The author traces a linear trajectory of this phenomenon in Mootoo's work, situating the horrors of abuse with those described by Indo-Caribbean female narratives such as those of Ramabai Espinet and Lakshmi Persaud within Indo-Caribbean religious and cultural memories and furthered by the emasculation of indentureship in the Caribbean. Mootoo does not leave the Indo-Caribbean male irredeemable, but creates alternate Indo-Caribbean males to balance her representations of the negative stereotypes. Thus, the horrors she narratively witnesses, are counterbalanced with hopeful counter figures.

Asma Sayed's "Postcolonial Ecologies and Sustainable Living: Reading Jenna Butler's Nonfiction" adds an ecocritical dimension to this collection of essays. Sayed engages contemporary postcolonial ecocritical theory to make an in-depth study of Jenna Butler's eco-conscious narratives and her lifestyle. Sayed demonstrates how Butler's works are important to Canadian environmental literature and the literature of the environment. In her writing and her lifestyle Butler protests against the European settler-colonialist extractivist mentality, which has damaged the biosystems of all the lands they conquered. She rejects the current biocentric and anthropocentric way of life and proposes moving towards sustainability based on a philosophy of ecocentrism.

In the final essay of this volume, Dannabang Kuwabong draws attention to Claire Harris's role as a poetic witness to the social malaises founded on systems of violence presided over by the powerful the world over. Harris understands passionately how these systems of domination traumatize people of every gender, class, ethnicity, and generation. The essay reveals the complexity of Harris's poetic architecture, employing word and line arrangements, allusions, literary collage, white spaces, intertextuality, and fragmentariness. Harris targets all women, interrogating the hidden biases that prevent women from realizing the politics of universal sisterhood to battle systems of domination. Her engagement of sociological data and history sustains her lament. These poems are Harris's testimonies against societal complacencies in the face of the evils of racism, classism, colorism, ethnocentrisms, domestic violence, war, pedophilia, medical malpractices, patriarchy, global capitalism that prefers profit over human and environmental rights, and corrupt legal and religious systems.

Confluences 3: Essays on the New Canadian Literature should appeal to all interested in broadening their minds about what it would look like if these new works of literature are embraced, studied, and included in the canon, not to replace what is already there, but to expand it. The series also establishes a flexible channel to hear other voices and learn about the new literature of Canada.

—Dannabang Kuwabong

PAMELA MORDECAI

Pamela Mordecai's Literary Transcultural Eschatology

Dannabang Kuwabong

> Female voices
> (Addressing the audience.) Listen, crowd-o-people! Tune in to dis heartbreak story! Walk a short way wid dis Sistren. Help her bear her load. (*de book of Mary: A Performance Poem* 1)

> NAOMI
> Oonu see mi dying trial!
> Dem people yah nuh easy.
> A kill dem a go kill de man.
> How yu mean "Which man?"
> Nuh de man Jesus. Yuh know.
> (*de Man: A Performance Poem* 9)

Pamela Mordecai is one of the leading Jamaican Canadian writers, who has written, edited, and published over thirty books of poetry, fiction, drama, and culture. Her work spans across a wide range of themes and genres targeting junior, young-adult, and adult readers. Her first book, *Jamaica Woman*, co-edited with Mervyn Morris, appeared in 1980, and *Red Jacket: a novel*, shortlisted for the Rogers Writers' Trust Fiction Award, and *de book of Mary: A Performance Poem* both were released in 2015. Yet, though often listed among Canadian and Caribbean women writers, her work has yet to receive any serious scholarship. This essay is my response to Naomi's cry "oonu see [her] dying trial," my way of walking "a short way wid dis Sistren / help her bear her load" at the fringes of Caribbean-Caribbean literary studies.

Mordecai's *Journey Poem* (1987) launched her debut entry to the well-policed group of Jamaican poets in the latter twentieth century. She emigrated to Canada in 1994; a year later, in 1995, she published *de Man: a performance poem.* Portions of this dramatic poem were performed before a predominantly European Canadian (or white) Catholic congregation on Good Friday and got a standing ovation for its fresh representation of the *Passion of Jesus: Certifiable: Poems* (2001); *Pink Icing: stories* (2006); *Subversive Sonnets* (2012); R*ed Jacket, a novel* (2015) and *de book of Mary* (2015). In this essay, I focus on how Mordecai explores her Catholic Christianity in three books: *de Man: a performance poem, de book of Mary: A Performance poem*, and *Red Jacket: a novel.* I show that Mordecai's poetry and fiction entreats a reader or audience participation; they are presented as readerly texts that appropriate Jamaican folklore and theatre. I read *de Man: a performance poem* and *de Book of Mary A Performance Poem* as performative adaptations of biblical stories. All are eschatological narratives based on a Caribbean Christian theology of salvation. The stories engage Caribbean cultural, linguistic, spiritual, historical, and public spaces to formulate an African Caribbean Christian ethos.They do not exhibit the stereotypical denunciations of Christianity presented in the works of her contemporaries. Thus, despite her recognition of how the Bible was used to enforce slavery, segregation, racism, sexism, and toxic masculinity in the Caribbean, she nonetheless asserts her faith in Jesus.

In *Ruin the Sacred Truths: Poetry and Belief from the Bible to the Present*, the critic Harold Bloom claims that although "Poetry and belief . . . [present] antithetical modes of knowledge, . . . [they] share the peculiarity of taking place *between* truth and meaning, while being somewhat alienated both from truth and from meaning" (12). Bloom defends this potentially contradictory position by contending that meanings in both poetry and belief are initiated and constructed in performative excesses and organized around and through symbolic repetitions of sound, word, imagery, ritual, etc., without which, he declares, "even poetry, let alone belief, is merely a mode of repetition, no matter how much finer a tone" (12). Citing John Milton, Bloom further argues that such a combination of contradictory engagements in poetry and belief generates "vitalism and theomorphism," which become agents of "transumption gorgeously expanding the Bible or displacing it through extraordinary condensation and perspectivizing" (93). Bloom cites W B C Watkins's supposition that argues that with Milton, "we cannot overstress a fundamental truth about . . . [his work] which we find endlessly proliferated . . . the physical, specifically the senses, to the ultimate Divine as *absolutely unbroken* . . . [he] is free to speak of any order of being . . . in identical sensuous terms as the great denominator" (Bloom 94). Bloom concludes: "A poet who believes in so much that is transcendent . . . does not often conceive of the transcendent as being apprehended by our fallen senses" (Bloom 94).

Bloom's theory influences my position. I content that in Mordecai's *de Man: a performance poem* (1995), *de book of Mary* (2015), *Subversive Sonnets* (2012), *Certifiable* (2001), and her ambitious novel, *Red Jacket* (2015), the author "transumes every extra poetic belief" in contemporary Christianity (Bloom 96). Mordecai, to borrow Bloom's description of Milton, "stations [herself], with radical originality, in an anxiously emptied-out present time, between a culturally wealthy but error-laden past and a weirdly problematic future" (Bloom 96). Mordecai's vitalism casts out dualistic interpretations and practice of faith to render fresher and challenging ways of recasting New Testament stories from her Jamaican roots for the Caribbean and global audiences. Mordecai's poetic relevance as a Canadian author rises from her originality, which sets her apart from other Caribbean Canadian authors who are often consumed with issues of the contradictions of multiculturalism, racism, etc. Mordecai's work ranks among the (in)visible non-Euro-Canadian cultural insurgents from among a larger Caribbean diaspora intervention in Canada's literary landscape. She reveals how the impact of her migration to Canada informs her recent poetry and fiction. Savory writes; "Diaspora and the transnational are not only grounded in realities of migrations and their impact on the people who experience them, but also in definitions of nation which are key to both the colonial projects of Europe and the reactive post-colonial necessity of defining it anew" (95). Mordecai's relocation in Canada, after her sojourns in other places, creates challenges of integration, retention, and redefinition of her cultural identities through adaptations. An established cultural creator and activist, Mordecai brought aspects of the Creole identities that inform Jamaican national consciousness to successfully negotiate her presence in Canada. Cordelia Forbes observes that the cultural flexibility of diaspora Caribbean people, constructed from their creolization, has given them greater freedom to define themselves in the dominant Eurocentric metropolises (21).

As "[a]ll strong poets must ruin the sacred truths to fable and old song, precisely because the essential conditions for poetic strength is that the new song, one's own, always must be strong of one's self... (Bloom 125), Mordecai "ruins" New Testament Biblical narratives, as often presented through a Eurocentric Catholic Christian liturgy, by retelling them through Jamaican voices. She ruins the imagined sacredness of Canadian poetry and Canadian Catholic orthodoxy by introducing a Jamaican style of irreverence in language (Patois) and themes and disturbing the serenity of dominant Euro-Canadian literary and religious landscapes. While following the pattern of medieval miracle plays staged in Canadian Catholic churches and schools at Christmas and Easter liturgical services, which emphasize Christian hope and apocalypse, Mordecai adds an African Caribbean dimension through inculturation and theological reinterpretations of that faith to reignite public debates about Christianity among Canadian and Caribbean audiences.

Mordecai asserts that "Religion has turned into such an ugly word. So many irreligious things have been done in its name! I believe in Jesus. I like him. He was a rebel, bent on upsetting the status quo. He is my kind of guy and so I am interested in his story" (Mordecai, 2019). Her view of Mary is expressed in similarly glowing terms: "She was an adventurous fourteen-year-old with a lot of spunk. The situation of this mother and son, colonized as they were at the time by the downpressive Romans, is not unlike my own. I grew up in an island colonized by the British, also downpressors" (Mordecai, 2019). Recognizing the parallel histories of Mary and herself, Mordecai goes on to address how language is engaged to hierarchize Canadian and Caribbean societies along with class and race: "The language situations are also similar: in Jesus' time, important folks spoke one way, and poor folks spoke another. In Jesus' case, Latin and Hebrew were the prestige languages and Aramaic and Koine Greek the dialects; in my case, English was the `standard' language and

Jamaican Creole or Patwa the dialect" (Mordecai, 2019). Thus, her choice of Jamaican Patois as her poetic and narrative medium aligns her with the ordinary, marginalized people of Jamaica and Canada, who form the bulk of her audience. Her choice of language is also bolstered by the Second Vatican Council's policy of inculturation in the Catholic Church to make Jesus' gospel of peace and love meaningful in different cultures.

Inculturation underpins Mordacai's bold retelling of New Testament stories through translational and transcultural adaptations that expand on the historical contents of the stories and roots them firmly in the cultural and historical landscape of Jamaica. Mary's story, one of maternal suffering, often silenced in Church liturgy, is reconceived culturally and filtered through a Caribbean womanist and maternal prism. It challenges male-dominated Christian eschatology and opens spaces for a discussion of motherhood and male oppression of women, domestic and social violence against women, male irresponsibility, and historical erasures of women's voices. It justifies Catholic extrabiblical reverence of Mary through which she is seen as co-redemptory with Jesus. The women narrators in *de book of Mary* share similar experiences with Mary. They too suffer from motherhood woes, loneliness and rejection, and patriarchal oppression, yet they remain faithful to God. Their appeal to a skeptical male audience, who dismissively call Mary's role in Christianity, "A mythic tale, you hear, / not a thing, but make-up / herstory" (*De Book of Mary*... 1), sets the stage to demonstrate Mary's pivotal role in the birth of Christianity.

Mordecai's story of Mary humanizes Mary. It exposes the historical, religious, and cultural issues of patriarchy, motherhood, immigration, political terrorism, colonialism, loneliness, and friendship. She is inextricably woven into Jesus' story, which often is forgotten in Christian eschatology. In both *de Man* and *de book of Mary*, Mordecai runs parallel stories: 1. divine intervention in human affairs in agreement with human free will; 2. human suffering under unjust human laws; 3. unfulfilled love, sociopolitical and gender oppression, dislocation, and violence. Gabriel reveals how what is often alluded by men to God are inventions by men, "who too love to take / tings and twist to dem suit" to present God as a dictator, unwilling to reason with humans. Instead, Mordecai presents God as a merciful being willing to form alliances with humans. "Am-Who-Am-Over-All, De-Great One- / Who-Run-Tings, say is choose" that Mary must make (*de book of Mary* . . . 11). Mary is given a chance by God to exercise her free will in His salvation plan for humanity.

The angel Gabriel in *de book of Mary* presents heaven where ". . . every angel above / in de heavenly host would quick give / dem eye-teeth to bear dis Holy Ghost begot child!" (15) in order to convince Mary to say yes. She, however, is conflicted with the idea. She wonders how it would affect her mother and Joseph within the larger society still ruled by Mosaic Law. Gabriel insists that if Mary reflects on the Torah carefully she will realize that she is the virgin in Isaiah's prophecy to King Ahab: "Therefore the Lord himself shall give you a sign; Behold, a virgin shall conceive, and bear a son, and shall call his name Immanuel" (Isaiah 7:14). Because this is God's will for the future of humanity, Mary must boldly discount the Old Testament legalisms that severely curtail and control female sexuality (Deut. 22:14-29). When Mary's Pa and Ma consult a priest in the Temple, he answers that El Shaddai says, "Never mind old time ways, never mind / how she young, woman not nobody property. / She free to decide on her own destiny" (*de book of Mary* 16). Neither Gabriel nor Mordecai imply that Mary's acceptance to be the unwed mother of Jesus will easily be accepted by her mother, Anne, or her betrothed, Joseph (*de book of Mary* 32). She wonders how ". . . [she] going to recount / dat to Ma? Or to Pa? Or Joseph? / Never mind how me try?" (32). Mary's action could shame her mother and undermine Joseph's masculinity in public. If her belly starts swelling, "wicked folks / bound to find things to chew" (16). Their malicious minds and spite make them "wallow in dem fellow man bad luck, / rejoice when disaster fall on dem!" (16). Mary faces a greater dilemma when after asking God in prayer to help her make the right choice. God remains silent: "And me listen but Jah-Jah not saying nothing / Verily he leaving de matter up to me. / So me use my good sense and me make a wager" (17). The wager: "Please tell Him-Who-Run-Things / I glad him choose me" (17). When God refuses to guide her to choose a yes or no to His invitation, it gives Mary the space needed to use her free will.

The second scene of the book critiques the masculinist interpretation of Christianity through Mosaic legalism, which justifies the subordination of women either by appealing to Deuteronomic laws or Paul's declaration that wives must be submissive to husbands, as cited in Ephesians 5:22-23. Unsurprisingly, when the men notice Mary is pregnant, and that Joseph is not the father but has accepted custody of the child, they condemn Joseph's stand. They mock him, "Better Joseph than any of we! / you would think a man quick / wid him carpentry hand" they mockingly state, "would have intelligence in him head!" (36). They reject Joseph's courage and generosity of spirit and decide that in "no way we would married any woman / . . . / wid a next man pikni big / in her belly." For in their human logic, "Nobody want no / jacket in dem family" (37). The question is, who creates the jacket that a real thinking man is so anxious to reject? They cannot understand God's plans for human salvation through Christianity, brought up as they are on the Mosaic laws that are set out in Deuteronomy 22: 13 -16. Even Joseph at a point debates whether to follow the law of Moses and expose Mary to be stoned to death for her sin (34) or secretly disown her and walk away. In her confusion, Mary mounts a vigorous plea. She laments that her lowly socioeconomic status and having no political connections, she does not expect to receive any clemency from the hardhearted and legalistic crowd. She contends with God for the protection of His baby even if He does not care for her anymore. If she is killed, then His baby she is carrying will also be killed. Mary symbolizes ordinary Jamaicans and Canadians who are caught in the web of legalism with no one to speak on their behalf for small infractions that hurt nobody.

The men are so addicted to a strict adherence to the violent interpretation of Mosaic Law that like the forefathers, they reject Jesus' new teaching of love and forgiveness. The women in amazement exclaim, "Jesus long come and gone. Him did bring / a new Law. It say de likes of you / do not own none of we? Except through violence: You lot not no better. You all love violence / Dem cut your navel string / on disruption and war" (38). Stung to the core, the men threaten the women with violence and justify it concerning their history of violence against women. Thus, while discussing the story of Mary, Mordecai inserts social protest in the perennial and multiple levels of violence against women. The rest of the book focuses on Mary's life after the day of Pentecost. Since very few of those years of Mary are in the Bible, Mordecai draws evidence from

The Protoevangelium of James and *The Infancy of Thomas*, apocryphal texts that contain more details about Mary and gives the story greater verisimilitude.

de book of Mary addresses contemporary gender-based oppression. It challenges the erasure of Mary's centrality in Christian eschatological narratives. This challenge irks the men, and so the women ask, "Don't know why Mary story annoy / you so much? / Is your conscience, maybe? Is because" it reveals their shame (Mordecai 36). Whether it is about Mary or Jesus, the men feel ill at ease. In the end, they tell the men that since the problem with men is that they have no idea about motherhood and mothering as a parenting practice, they should shut up. If they knew about parenting, they would know that a mother's story is not separate from her child(ren) (116-117). The women praise Mary's courage in her willingness to accept to be the unwed mother of Jesus, irrespective of the possible terrifying consequences. Failing to find fault with the women's position, the men attack their intelligence and blame unashamedly Jesus' subversive sermons that have undermined the cultural and religious construction of gender inequality in which women are subordinated. They lament that if not for Jesus, "womanlike all-o-you / would never lose dem pass interfere / in matters beyond what dem pea-brain" can process (119). Failing to silence the women, they use threats of violence to cow the women. The men are unhappy that true Christian spirituality liberates all from oppressive laws. They resort to the hackneyed refrain that justifies male rule in all matters by appealing to ancient laws that have been claimed to have been given by an unchanging God: "Man is man. Man in charge. / So Jehovah ordain. / So de Torah declare" (120). They declare that Jesus is dead and gone. And men still rule things. The women challenge men to tell them what they will do about female freedom. Lacking anything to say, the men resort again to attacking Jesus' message of love, forgiveness, and neighbourliness, which seriously undermines male power. Realizing the mental block preventing the men from accepting the new reality, the women leave them with a Jamaican proverb: "Old folks say you can lead / Jackass go a water" but that if the Jackass refuses to drink, you cannot force him. The men are the jackasses in this case who are led to see the truth and be set free of their ignorance. They then leave, with the women taunting, "you lot / . . . /

And jackass . . . Have good resemblance" (121). The women's concluding remarks echo Jesus' criticism of the Jewish leaders who have continually criticized and rejected all the prophets sent by God to them. The women have "piped to" the men and they "have refused to dance," and they "have mourned to [them] and [they] have not wept . . ." (Luke 7:32-35). Frustrated, therefore, the women call the men jackasses.

de book of Mary provides Mordecai the space to draw attention to gender inequality and the importance of women's roles and voices in Christian evangelization. Nalo Hopkinson perceptively affirms, "Mordecai (re)claims and re-centers the story of Maiden Mary, triumphantly transposing it from the word of men to the stories of women, and from High Church language to everyday speech . . . [S]he performs the legacy of Caribbean creolization [with] a . . . hybrid . . . [of] . . . Greek theatre, . . . Judaism, and the beauty of Caribbean vernaculars and sensibilities" (as quoted on back cover of the book). Mordecai's women in proclaiming Jesus before men, insert women's voices as pertinent to Christian evangelization. The men who refuse to accept Jesus' message, symbolize humans who refuse the message of love and peace and stick to their old ways. Jesus's words are enacted by the women to evangelize: "Whomsoever shall confess me before men him shall the Son of man also confess before the angels of God. / But he that denieth me before men shall be denied before angels of God" (Luke 12: 8-9). Mordecai proclaims Jesus through Mary's story before men. The men deny and reject the truth even though it is prophesized in the Torah.

Mordecai's *de Man* (1995) received excellent reviews for its eschatological freshness on stage in both Canada and Jamaica. It secured for Mordecai a place among Christian poets in both countries. It is an "eyewitness account by two observers who are participants-by-extension, of the crucifixion of Jesus Christ" (back cover) One is Naomi, "a middle-aged woman and a maid in the service of Pontius Pilate's wife," sent by her mistress to witness what is happening to Jesus and bring back an eyewitness account. The other, an old and disabled Samuel who was taught carpentry by Joseph and has now come to witness with sympathetic understanding the passion of the little boy Jesus he knew "running up and down chasing him bull in Nazareth" (27-28). Both render their accounts in Jamaican demotic. Elaine Savory has articulated that Canada provided the cultural laxity and space to facilitate the writing, performance, publication, and acceptance of Jesus' passion story in Patwa. This may not have been possible in Jamaica in 1995. It was still considered blasphemous to translate Catholic liturgy into Caribbean creole despite Vatican II's policy of inculturation. Savory writes, "What Mordecai has in Canada is the space of migration, in which her imagination can freely explore aspects of Jamaica, and ways of portraying it, space which has proved to be a rich resource for many other Caribbean writers" (Savory112). The benefits are two-way: "What Canada has in Mordecai is a strongly humanist voice, unafraid of difficult subjects and always willing to pursue new imaginative and linguistic horizons" (112). Though such a notion of transnational interculturality is still illusory for most immigrant writers in Canada, the positive reception of the poem even in the mid-1990s was a breakthrough.

Obedient to Vatican II's policy of inculturation, Mordecai employs Jamaican creole to nativize the liturgy of Jesus' passion. She defends her choice of Jamaican creole to proselytize through poetry: "Bible translators . . . speak of a community's 'heart language.' Creole is my heart language . . . Creole gives me poems and stories in a way that English does not. Writing in Creole is also a political decision" (Mordecai 2019). Additionally, this political stand emanates from her determination to bring to voice and "affirm and celebrate perhaps the first thing that the enslaved peoples of Africa made when they were stolen from their homes and forcibly transported to an alien and brutal island world where every effort was made to dehumanise them and strip away their languages and cultures" (2019). A Caliban in Prospero's Canada, Creole gives her voice. This realization she claims, dawned on [her] while [she] was writing de Man (Mordecai 188): "The voice is Caliban's voice; the language used for cursing, with all the ironies that imply. The glossolalic syllables . . . and the making of Pan . . . are resonant symbols for me. Pan is a voice we have made. Creole is a language we have made. Calypso [Reggae] is a music we've made" (188). Not only language but the formulaic opening in the oral storytelling tradition, especially tragic stories in Jamaica, also informs Naomi's exclamatory opening: "Oonu see mi dyin trial!" (*de Man* 9) The statement reflects a formulaic opening to Jamaican narratives of woe and elicits the sympathetic attention of the youth audience.

Like Jesus, her cross is imposed by a higher authority which she must carry. Her mistress, the wife of Pontius Pilate, sends her out to witness and report back to her on the trial and crucifixion of Jesus. Her experience as an eyewitness to an execution of an innocent man, and one who did so much for ordinary people, is as traumatizing as Jesus' passion.

de Man, I contend, is Mordecai's challenge to the Catholic Bishops of Jamaica and Canada to accept Jamaican creole to be as good a language for Catholic liturgical services and Bible translation as any language, following Vatican II. She issued a challenge that claimed that the theology of inculturation includes, "the incarnation of Christian faith in myriad cultural contexts" (Wielzen 108), and that included Jamaican language and culture. Mordecai's *de Man*, together with other such publications, as Anna Kasafi Perkins indicates, "resurfaced [and challenged the] national debate about the value of the Jamaican language and its appropriateness for speaking, much less reading and writing. And to translate the Bible into Jamaican is tantamount to blasphemy" (26). The 2008 decision by the Jamaican Catholic Bishops to translate the New Testament into Creole confirmed Mordecai's position, and hence she stands as a pioneer in using Jamaican Creole to create poetry for evangelization. In *de Man* and *de Book of Mary*, Mordecai engages linguistic choices to assert a Caribbean cultural collective consciousness and instigate theological defiance through a hermeneutic and an "ideographic remonstration" from which she disturbs, unlocks, liberates, and memorializes Caribbean Christian narrative dogma hitherto dominated by Eurocentrism (Griffith 17). Here engagement of Jamaican orality and cultural references generates polyvalent alterity through which she stages an ambivalent counteraction against intolerance in Christian eschatology and theology (18). The poems reveal sociocultural mutability and resilience that ultimately amplify and define what it means to 'inculturate' the bible into Jamaican culture.

Naomi's dialogue with Jamaican youth, who are largely oblivious to the history of their faith and of injustice on the island, sets the stage for exploring the crucifixion story of Jesus, as the story of hope for the voiceless oppressed. Mordecai transnationalizes and transculturates the happenings in Jerusalem of 2021 years ago to contemporary Jamaica and Canada. The incredulity of the youth that such an important story has escaped their notice, encourages Naomi to educate and evangelize them about the man Jesus (*de Man* 9). Mordecai links evangelization to history. She gives Naomi and Samuel the wisdom to link the past as represented in the cruel crucifixion of Jesus, to present religious, political, economic, and social injustices that underwrite the suffering of the marginalized. In the process, she formulates her Caribbean Christian ethos, one that stands in stark contrast to the predominant anti-Christian ethos of the majority of Caribbean writers. To Nigel Thomas's comment on how "a Caribbean ethos... informs" her writing, even with those set outside Jamaica, Pamela Mordecai responds with a brief history of how attending a Catholic school in Kingston during the Colonial period spared her "the full colonial brainwashing that many... were subjected to" because Catholic schools did not have to teach British history to their students; furthermore, "the school... stressed the performing arts, with a strong Jamaican focus," in which there was both the stress for indigenous theatre with "sections in the speech festival for the performance of dialect poetry" (178). *de Man*, therefore, is Mordecai's transcultural translation of Catholic ritual and liturgical re-enactment of the imagined fourteen stations of the cross enumerated every Good Friday to cover Jesus' arrest and journey from the Garden of Gethsemane to Golgotha where he is crucified on the Cross. Though performed in a language foreign to the Canadian congregation, Mordecai is not surprised that the "response was overwhelming – very much as if the congregation was hearing the story for the first time" (178). Mordecai asserts: "... there are ways of making people pay attention to song and story ... Literature is an excellent tool for helping us to understand... who we are and what we have, and how much more we can do" (180). She further asserts that her work "... serves as celebration and entertainment and instruction, whether they are of Caribbean heritage or otherwise... The elements are there: humour, rhyme, rhythm, story... sometimes even music... it's a celebration for my audiences ... if what's familiar and treasured on the part of the Caribbean [or Christian] people, and of what is energetic, honest and earthy on the part of non-Caribbeans" (182). As a corollary to the above, Griesinger argues that because "literature can expose the ugliness of oppression and injustice experienced by ethnic minorities within a multicultural" Christian West, "one of the eschatological functions of literature is to keep creation moving in the right direction, a task requiring a good deal more alignment with Christ and his purposes that typify the field of literary studies today" (217).

Thus, in *de Man*, Mordecai chooses to focus on what Volf calls Jesus' "preferential option for the powerless" on the cross. Jesus' action "implies a privileged hearing for those whose voices are excluded" (213), such as is manifested in the ignorance of the youth. Mordecai's poem is her contribution to exposing and denouncing this ignorance that breeds moral laxity and evil, in which the inaction of the Church is a form of acceptance by her hierarchy. The ecstatic eruption of the audience in the Canadian school where she performed sections of *de Man* was prophetic in recognition because "I think because they'd never heard anything like it before" (Mordecai 182). For Mordecai, her vision that ". . . that literature is the place where God makes his last stand, so to speak" (187) comes true. Mordecai realizes that *de Man* and *de book of Mary*, "apart from illuminating the present, especially our need for salvation, and preserving the past, . . . contributes to the divine project by anticipating, foreshadowing, and luring us toward the future" (218). Mordecai's transcultural interpretation and re-enactment of Jesus' Passion creates and fulfills these three aspirations with the newness of perspective for a Canadian audience bored with the stuffy old ways of telling these stories. *de Man* helps the audiences in both Jamaica and Canada to reassess their faith through the eyes of others who have been rejected because they are different. It shows that Christianity can be reinvigorated through transcultural and translingual poetics.

Mordecai extends her vision about the need to translate and acculturate her faith practices through Jamaica language poetry. She asserts that because " 'Caribbeans'" come here aware at some level that we have the task of what Louise Bennett calls `Colonization in Reverse,' we bring plenty; we don't come with our two long, empty hands. In *Certifiable*, Serafina the health worker declares unabashedly that she hears from God's messenger, "never mind he arrives in an odd form. When the incontinent white patient . . . joins battle with her, she routs him with her rhetoric and Bible knowledge" (Mordecai 178). Impudently, Serafina tries to preach Jesus to this aged white Canadian male whom she is caring for and gets sacked for her daring. She has been preaching apocalyptic messages that she claims she receives from a squirrel. A bedridden quarrelsome bitter white male she takes care of mocks her with the question, "Is it that all Black folks are dumb/ / believers in this silly stuff?'" or is Serafina suffering from an irredeemably uncultivated and ill-mannered mindset (87). Serafina cites Corinthians 1: 1 in her response: "It dealeth with the likes / of you. The Lord shall bring to nought / the wisdom of ones who think "they are knowledgeable about the world," especially "... all those that bedridden / and cannot control nor piss nor poo / them bold to bring contention to all who [are healthy]" (87). Mordecai argues that Serafina's "triumph of being even after she is fired and jobless, her act of claiming who she is, her Christian spirituality" gives her the assurance of peace in Jesus as articulated in the poem "Blessed Assurance," in which faith in Jesus gives comfort to those who are downpressed and marginalized in Canadian society (188). In several poems in *Certifiable* and *Subversive Sonnets*, Mordecai challenges us to become "sensitive to what God is doing cross-culturally and celebrat[e] stories that raise consciousness about cultures other than our own. Surely literature has a role to play in helping us to imagine the suffering of people who are different from us" (Griesinger 226). Serafina's vision of God is symptomatic of Mordecai's interrogation of first, Canada's multiculturalism policy, and second, the Catholic Church's claim to inculturate, both of which lack any seriousness, being devoid of cultural inclusivity and plural perspectivity outside European paradigms. "Serafina" is Mordecai's assertion that Caribbean immigrants to Canada do not just bring their cultures and languages, but most importantly, are unafraid to speak about God from their cultural and historical locations. We are compelled therefore to see how Caribbean people inhabit and exhibit their Caribbean Christianity as animated by her historical, racial, gender, class, and locational realities.

Mordecai asserts that what triggered her was a revelatory awareness that Jesus, as he walked and preached, was not speaking to the people in highfalutin Hebrew or Latin or Greek, but in Aramaic, the language of the commoners and the marginalized, as most Jamaicans are in Canada. Thus, the cultural and linguistic compass that directed her poetic journey in *de Man*, *Certifiable*, *Subversive Sonnets*, and *de Book of Mary* is the language, and socioeconomic location of the people for whom and with whom she writes. Samuel relates how, when he loses his arm, it is Joseph and Mary who take him in. It is Joseph who teaches him to be an excellent carpenter and mason. In observing the comment on Jesus' suffering, Samuel and Naomi both develop emotional affiliations with Jesus. They recall their unfulfilled love—prevented from marrying and forced to live separate and celibate lives , they live with regrets only. The upper classes hide behind arcane Mosaic Laws to live out their ambitions for power. Jealousy, corruption, greed, and megalomania dominate the minds of the leaders and generate hatred for Jesus, who taught and lived differently. Hence Samuel refuses to see Jesus' suffering and death as signaling despair. Rather, he sees it as salvific. Jesus' death is a sacrifice of redemption, Golgotha is the altar, and "de man Jesus is de / Offering . . ." (*de Man* 58-59). For Samuel, the "story of Jesus Christ [is] the unfolding revelation of the Hebrew God of the Old Testament—the God of promise" (Griesinger 215) and embodies the hope of transforming and transfiguring our past, present, and future toward perfection. This embodied hope is evident in Christ, the crucified God in human flesh. Christ must suffer and die an inglorious death to save us from the power of Satan and human sinfulness. Samuel and Naomi do not see this as crucified hope ending in despair, but epiphanically as an investment in a sacramental future when they and other silenced and marginalized people will have a hearing before God.

Samuel's epiphany empowers him to choose to follow Jesus and not the self-centered and oppressive teaching of the priests. He promises to follow only genuine priests: "Today me / Must find out which priest is / Really priest" and search for the priest "Who have de truth, who have / De power, who me must / Follow –the Pharisee dem," or as he puts it, "de Nazarene" (*de Man* 59). Both Naomi's and Samuel's resolve become an invitation to seek God with renewed zeal, and not just follow what false Church leaders teach (62). Their resolve is strengthened by the supernatural events that presage the death of Jesus: the darkening of the sun, the earthquake, and the escape of duppies from graves testify to Jesus' supernaturality. Naomi's proclamation that she will follow Jesus whether he was divine or not is irrelevant to matters of faith. What she knows is that Jesus, "Was a special child / Fi true. Me nuh know if / Him was God son, Messiah" (73). She has no doubt, "Dat Jesus not no ordinary man" (73) and did no one any harm. He preached only peace, forgiveness, love, and healed the sick, raised the dead, and prophesized goodwill to all (62). Through Samuel and Naomi, Mordecai advocates that to follow Jesus, one "Best learn to study peace. / Yuh, me, de Roman dem / De Pharisee, stranger / Familiar, family" (76). All must live in peace and love with each other (76). To Naomi and Samuel, Jesus came to save not to destroy, as he proclaims in Luke 7: 34.

Mordecai claims that by maintaining the cadence of Jamaican language throughout the poem, she is united to the poem: "the poem in Jamaican language unites me . . . it's a mistake to think of Creole as a vehicle for just belly-laugh humour, puns, double entendre, sarcasm, irony – these are all devices that the vernacular employs, Jamaican proverbs . . . writ language as strands weaves image into image across poems" (Batcos 58). Batcos, writing about Olive Senior, claims that "to write for a broad range of listeners, [she] also engages herself constantly as well as overtly with an audience of Caribbean origin to fulfill an aesthetic – both individually and compound—embedded in the Jamaican oral tradition of [dramatic] storytelling" (58), This applies equally to Pamela Mordecai. Through Creole, as both a specific cultural icon and metaphor of her transcultural mobility in Canada, Mordecai destabilizes, as Glissant has argued, the philosophy of fixed rootedness, spatiality, temporality, and identity (2). Stuart Hall persuasively extends this argument to show that Caribbean identity must be addressed from multiple lenses, whose collage or kaleidoscope of signs and positions depend upon interlocking variables such as culture, class, political ideology, spirituality, gender, location, history, and language (3). In her poetry Mordecai articulates her Christian Catholic identity from multiple locations. She does not sacrifice her faith in the name of literary feminism or postcolonial religious stances that seduce Caribbean writers into masquerade dances with superficial affiliations to African-derived spiritualities that few can practice or care to fully embrace.

Mordecai's refusal therefore to derogate the Catholic faith, which she claims made her who she is, is a welcome departure. Her recognition of the positive roles of nuns in Jamaican society is illuminating. Nuns are saviors of orphans. The twelve orphan girls in "Lace Makers" (*Subversive Sonnets*, 7) are taught skills to become independent women or good wives and mothers someday. Yes, Reverend Mother Luke does not countenance the fun these girls have at the expense of Sister Mercedes, whose attempts to "talk Jamaican with her funny accent and first tongue" (7), generate laughter, but Mordecai's representation of the reverend mother is a parody of the stereotypical representations of nuns as unloving and domineering racist witches who traumatize the girls in convent schools. Missionary work to her is a chore, a sacrifice, not a calling(7). Believing that her idea of missionary work is shared by Sister Mercedes, she berates the girls for not reverencing the sister with fawning gratitude. Unlike Mother Luke, Sister Mercedes's relationship with her wards is reciprocal. She constantly foils and undermines Mother Luke's unreasonable, unmotherly, and unchristian sternness and actually enjoys her newfound freedom among Jamaicans. To her, Jamaica is home, Jamaicans are her people: "Dis is my home, / De sisters, you, my friends, de people here . . . all is my family. He take de blood / relations, yes. But see what bounty He / give me?" (8) She clearly understands Jesus' rebuke of his apostles when he tells them that they can approach God only as children (Luke 19: 13-14).

Unlike Sister Mercedes, Mother Luke is empty and materialistic minded; she is the "first woman in this while / island to drive a conveyance not pulled / by four-footed creatures" (Mordecai, *Subversive Sonnets* 8). She exhibits macho attributes, leaning "hard on the horn / of her red Ford . . . ," and with her skirt "slung in between her knees, beads furled into / her lap, dark glasses on her white bent nose, / she drive rough as any crafty truck man" (8). Unlike the gentle Jesus, she exacts severe corporal punishment for little infractions, taking literally the Old Testament advice: "He that spareth his rod hateth his son; but he who loveth him chastiseth him betimes" (Proverbs 13: 24). But Sister Mercedes reminds her of the New Testament: "Fathers, provoke not your children to anger, lest they be discouraged" (Col. 3:21).

Mother Luke, wielding the belt, is finally challenged by one of the girls, who rips the belt from her hands and flings it out the window, and publicly shames her. She calls into question the legitimacy of the title "Mother": "white lady, me / not fraid of you. Is you should shame! How you / could say you working in God's name while you" whip small girls mercilessly. Sister Mercedes concurs: "Luke, why you beat the child?

Look how long / been telling you beating don't do any good?" (9).

Mordecai's Catholic spirituality is much more positive, even as she recognizes the role of the Catholic Church in the racist and racialized history of the Caribbean and of Africa. Nonetheless, her vision of the positive aspects of the Church is based on her notion that grace, a gift of God, is enough to heal the wounds caused by evil. It is not Christ's teaching that is inimical to humans, but the way evil men and women have used the Bible and religion to establish dominion over others. Thus, she starts *Red Jacket* with the declaration: "Like all children of decent parents in the village, Grace raise in the Church. King James Version of The Holy Bible is the first book she ever see, the one book they read every day" (15). Grace's five-year-old mind may not have fully understood the words and allegorical significations of the stories. She engages the myth of Meshack, Daniel, and Abednego, three Hebrew youths who refused to worship the image of Nebuchadnezzar, to foreground Grace's story: "They trusted in him and defied the King's command and were willing to give up their lives rather than serve or worship any god except their own God" (Dan. 3:28). Mordecai suggests that African Caribbean Catholic spirituality does not imply a blind acceptance of clerical Eurocentric and racist interpretations of the Bible but must be culturally situated, informed, and sensitive to the Caribbean peoples' needs. Grace's Christianity is informed by Gramps's African Caribbean culture and worldview. "Gracie, I try to show you the difference between religion as a business and worshipping God in spirit and in truth, like the Bible say. If you are dealing with God in spirit and in truth, sometime you and him going to fuss. Ednis and her people mix up with a deity that give orders, count sins, and don't brook no argument" (65).

African Caribbean interpretation of the Bible contests and undermines this demoralizing and contradictory representation of God as a jealous, angry, and punitive male who brooks no questioning, unlike the loving forgiving God Jesus preached (145-6). To Grace, Gramps's relationship with God is more of a friendship, a negotiable understanding that humans and God need each other: "God give Gramps special permission to grow some plants that other people are forbidden to grow. God and Gramps are often scamps together, though if you are God, you couldn't be scamp" (33). To Grace, it, therefore, makes sense that God who makes the laws "could break them if [he] want" (34). It is comforting to know that "God change his mind and break his own rules, and it don't at all surprise that God should fie leave to do things others are not allowed to do. Gramps is special. God is smart so he would know" (34). Grace's logic reflects African Caribbean people's cultural interpretation of their relationship with the Christian God. Gramps, a cultural bridge between the African Caribbean spirituality and Christianity initiates Grace, and by extension Mordecai into a different type of Christian spirituality with an Africentric worldview.

Likewise, the engagement of African cultural and spiritual values enable Grace to accept her matrilineage, even if it is marred by incest. Grace's biological mother, Phillis, had been raped; when Grace denies assistance from Phillis, she learns a lesson. Phillis tells Grace: "Same thing or not, you can take my word about the blood business. Some African cultures have a concept of spiritual blood, something that's passed down through generations and contains the memory, history and wisdom of the tribe" (239). Even if Grace rejects consanguineous relationship with Phillis, she cannot abrogate the spiritual bonding that unites them in African Caribbean cosmology. The concept of ancestral spiritual bonding is further developed through Jimmy in *Red Jacket*. Jimmy, gifted with spiritual vision, enters the seminary to become a Catholic priest within the Jesuit order shortly after the death of his wife in the Alps. He misses the carnal pleasure his wife gave him. His unquenchable sexual desire troubles him. The Jesuits, like all Catholic clergy, are compelled to take vows of celibacy, which is a discipline, not a doctrine, that was enforced from about 1074 CE. It troubles Jimmy. He is afraid that this European injunction, which runs contrary to his African value about the importance of marriage, will frustrate his desire to be a good priest. He confesses this to his white superior, Reverend Father John Kelly (81-91). Kelly refers him to Joseph's struggle when he is forced to never touch Mary though they were married and tells Jimmy that such desires were not sinful, a position that undermines the Church's anti-sex injunctions.

Jimmy's conflicting relationship with the Church's rules on sex does not derail his calling into priesthood. Likewise, Grace finds that her Christian upbringing provides her the type of comforting security that secular academic theory and knowledge fail to provide in

Canada. Though she realizes the oppressive nature of the so-called Ten Commandments, Grace finds niches of solace in Church. She believes that things would not have turned out badly if she hadn't given up on an orphan child, at The Beloved Church in Toronto. The little boy's death at The Beloved's, her loneliness, and nostalgia develop into depression. She is desperate to find a church, a community of believers who could help console her. "She will ask someone, maybe the St Chris young women in the office at Rachan. She has no family nearby, not even distant kin, and she feels as if a bed of rockstone has just buried her. All she can think of is the St Chris remedy—talking to the Lord, which means Church" (*Red Jacket* 250).

This leads Grace to Newberry Hall, built by the Student Christian Association, as a former place of prayer meetings. She believes this discovery is a divine revelation and hence considers it hallow ground (251). The discovery of Newberry Hall becomes a confirmation of Gramps's words: "You don't find Church, Gracie! Church find you... So this is her church. She stops by almost every day, stares, considers, rails a little at Papa God. In time, she assembles a small group of four or five Caribbean fallen who meet here once a week for meditation" (251). Grace answers the call for Christian charity and lives out the gospel and salvation story of love. Her new-found faith is active and guides her altruism. She volunteers on weekends at Myrta's Home, a women's shelter. "She registers women and children, cooks and serves meals, make beds, does laundry, cares for babies, teaches literacy classes. It is at Myrta's that she loses her diffidence, thrust past it by the unabating stream of battered women and their children" (251). Her volunteerism is not out of misplaced spirituality or derived mechanically from human empathy. Her desire to work in a home for battered women derives from a nascent understanding of the Church's positive role in her life and that of her family. For Mordecai and Grace, the church, through many surrogate organizations and congregational associations formed by lay clergies and apostolates, performs great social functions that are aligned with Jesus' gospel message, "The Spirit of the Lord is upon me. He has sent me to liberate the enchained...," in Isaiah 61:1 and claimed by Jesus in his mission statement in Luke 4:16-19.

When Phyllis is raped at age fourteen by her stepbrother Raltson and conceives, it is the church of England that provides her with a cover story to enable her to leave the island in good standing. Aunt Evadine hides her at the home of girls with unwed pregnancy in Alton Mount. The Anglican Archdeacon Reverend Myers's wife runs the facility: "Well, Rev Myers say we will tell a kindly lie and say Phyllis is nearly fourteen. And till the baby come, because of the circumstances, Archdeacon Miller say he and Mrs Miller will have her in their own home, praise God for that" (278-279). Mordecai stresses this social gospel as the center of her religious faith. Her nuns fulfil these roles. Phyllis gives a positive narrative appraisal of her experience with nuns when she arrives in the United States, traumatized, and a confused and homeless new immigrant. The Religious Sisters of the Heart of Jesus in Our Lady of Good Hope Convent, New York, provide her sanctuary and a job. "The nuns were good to me from the beginning, and they operate a miraculous institution. They are mostly bright, talented women who love life and enjoy group service, and they have an excellent program. I have no desire to leave. . ." (3-5). When she collapses at her Aunt Vads funeral wake, these nuns take care of her: "Our sisters run a wonderful place called Mary's Heaven in Cohasset" (247-8). The love and care for Phyllis shown here and the role played by the Methodist Church and the Archdeacon of the Anglican Church testify to Mordecai's belief that not every action of the Christian Churches are traumatizing to African Caribbean people. She does not dwell on the terrible historical roles these churches played in African Caribbean peoples lives. Rather, she shows how these churches also play healing roles. This is a side of Christianity hardly elucidated in contemporary Caribbean literature.

Mordecai does not gloss over aspects of Christian worship that are insufficient in satisfying the needs of the faithful. In Toronto, Grace finds herself gradually disconnected from her Anglican spirituality, beginning with St Chad's in Wentley. She reflects on how at St Chad's, "God become distant, cold and, well, Anglican. Even if he exhale fire, God is lively in Wentley" (132). She decides to visit The Beloved Church to check out "whether God down there is jumping, or if he have a stiff upper lip" (132). Her earlier experience in the Aboriginal Church made her wary. Unbeknownst to her, "The Beloved Church . . . is in fact the Evangelical Church of the Father, Beloved Lord Jesus, and High Holy

Spirit. That sweet her no end. There and here can be the same, after all. It sweet her too that Rev Douglas, the pastor, is a woman. And plenty people from the Caribbean come there, so the congregation resemble one in Wentley" (132-13).

For a short period, Grace finds "Beloved" as a refuge. However, she soon stops going to church, not because she has a problem with the style of worship or with the congregation, but because she is consumed by her studies. When Christmas arrives, she feels the extreme loneliness in the European (white) Canadian environment. It is her roommate, Steph, a devout Catholic that comes to her rescue by inviting her to her home and where again she finds solace in the church. "That right find her at midnight Mass in Our Lady of Assumption Church in Peterborough, the one black lamb. When she look out and see snow to the nth power, she wonder again why she choose to be alien in this forbidding place" (134). Steph's Catholicism, though questioned by Grace's Evangelical holier-than-thou mindset initially as unchristian, has a resonance with Gramps's style of Christianity. Thus, when Steph relates how she and her mother have bet on a potted jade plant, Grace ruminates:

> So her roomie is a gambler too. That don't surprise her. Everybody know Catholics with their bingo and raffles. Lord have mercy! The Worshippers of Graven Images and Wearer of Evil Amulets is now also a what—Punter? Wagerer? Nor is that the end of it. Steph's iniquity extend in other directions as well, for she promise to take Grace to Allen Gardens to twitch a piece of public plant for Grace to grow in a private part of their room—on Gramps instruction and by his example. (121)

It is Gramps's type of Christianity that sees Grace through her college years, graduate studies, and finally, her dedication to working in a program to eradicate HIV/AIDS in Africa and other parts of the world. She finds spiritual bonding with Father Jimmy, and this is more rewarding to her than the casual attempt to fall in love with a womanizer. Finally, she understands her mother's idea that spiritual bonding is far greater than human sexual bonding, though they both seem to develop from the same place as the human need for fellowship. In Father Jimmy, she finds the type of love that is beyond sexual desire. At death, she gives her son to Reverend Jimmy to adopt as a son, what he had deeply desired with his wife but never achieved, and could not achieve biologically now, sworn as he is to celibacy and chastity.

Undoubtedly, the names Jimmy and Grace are symbolical. Mordecai confesses that the Protoevangelium of James provided her with extra information on the early lives of Mary and Jesus. Also, Grace is a reference to God's grace in her giving her son to Father Jimmy. And in adopting Grace's son, Jimmy plays the role that Joseph plays in the life of Jesus and Mary. At the end of the novel, we come away with a greater understanding of how for people of African and African Caribbean descent, the Catholic version of Christianity, especially its adherence to the social message of the Gospel, makes sense. As Birbalsingh has stated, "Perhaps it is not as strange as it looks that despite [Mordecai's] stern facing up to the grim reality of human oppression worldwide, Mordecai's poems express an underlying religious sensibility" (2). Her fiction and poetry ". . . reflect on [her] Jamaican (Caribbean) experience of social relations formed out of historic structures of slavery and their random enforced mixing of ethnic groups with differences of skin colour and cultural inheritance" (3).

This cultural créolité yields multiple adaptations through translanguaging, between transcultural landscaping, revisionary historicism, and constant adaptation and staticity in her religious poetry (Reiss 330). Adaptation nurtures shifting multiplicities and generates inculturation to enhance her narrative eschatology in her poetry. Savory contends, therefore, that Mordecai's Jamaica, had a history of "complex . . . cultural exchanges . . . [where] new oral forms have been created, developed, and finally exported" to Canada (96). This, as is evident, contributes to the long history of immigration which profoundly shape[s] Canada" (96). Adaptation is the ability, Savory says, to engage "the power of Jamaican language to make familiar religious icons new" (99) to a Canadian audience. Mordecai's claim for space in the Canadian literary landscape is recorded in the acknowledgment page of *Pink Icing and Other Stories* (2006). Her relationship to Christian spirituality is positive without eliding or glossing over the role of the Church in the racist and racialized history of the Caribbean.

All in all, Mordecai's poetry and fiction have added a new voice and vision to the landscape of Canadian literature. She has taken Canadian poetry back to a time when poets celebrated their Christian faith by embedding it in the literary landscape. Using poetry to participate in the call to a new evangelization, Mordecai joins other Canadian poets of faith such as John Terpstra and Margaret Atwood, but does so in her own way. She must be studied from that angle. Her work is intended to save Christianity from spiritual lethargy, insert multicultural perspectives into Canadian Christian life and in the process help decolonize it, expose the liberatory power of the gospel of Jesus; strengthen female voices and roles in Christian evangelization and liturgical performances; and open the door to the beauty of Christ's message and suffering over the ugliness of social evil. Mordecai's work has broken literary and spiritual boundaries, a welcome reenergization of Canadian literary and spiritual landscapes through orality and performance.

W H HUDSON AND PABLO URBANYI

W H Hudson's English Argentina And Pablo Urbanyi's Argentine Canada

Hugh Hazelton

The concept of national literatures has long been linked to the idea of linguistic homogeneity within a given geopolitical territory. There have also, however, been many instances that have run counter to this interpretation through the inclusion of dual or multiple linguistic and literary traditions within a single national literature. In older, more established nations such as Great Britain and Spain, which are themselves amalgams of different cultures and linguistic traditions, this has meant the inclusion of Scots and Galician as adjuncts to the national literatures in English and Spanish. In the newer countries of the Americas, however, the process of linguistic adaptation and cultural fusion has often been more dynamic, leading to the acceptance of writers in other languages than the dominant—whether immigrants, indigenous peoples, or bilingual individuals—as an integral part of the national literature, culture, and even identity. One has only to consider the importance of the Polish immigrant writer Witold Gombrowicz in Argentine letters; of Ole Rølvaag's *Giants in the Earth*, which is considered one of the great American novels of the settlement of the prairies, even though it was written in Norwegian; of the stature of the work of the Czech writer Josef Škvorecký in Canadian literature; or the work of indigenous peoples writing in their languages in countries throughout the Americas, especially in Mexico and the Andean countries.

The present study concentrates on two authors, one an Anglo-

American Argentine and the other an Argentine Canadian, who have established a major body of work in a language that is not that (or those, in the case of Canada) of their national literatures, and compares their reception both inside and outside their country of adoption. W H Hudson, a novelist, short-story writer, and naturalist who was born of American parents and raised in Argentina in the mid-nineteenth century, is considered an icon of Argentine culture, even though he wrote exclusively in English, and his work has been translated and integrated into the national literary canon. He is also, of course, a part of a long-standing Anglophone immigrant population in Argentina, which has made numerous other, though less noted, contributions to Argentine literature. Pablo Urbanyi, though born in Hungary and educated in Argentina, has spent over half his life in Canada, having settled in Ottawa after the Argentine coup d'état in 1976, and forms part of the Hispanic presence in Canadian literature. His work often deals directly with Canada and Canadian themes, yet, though it is widely respected and has been translated into English and French, it has not yet entered the literary mainstream of his second country. What explains the dichotomy in literary fortunes between the two writers in terms of their relative acceptance into the two national literatures? Why was Hudson's work able to enter Argentine national culture, while Urbanyi's writing, though warmly received in his home country, has met with a cooler reception in Canada?

W H Hudson was born in 1841, the fourth of six children, on a small estancia in the area near Quilmes, just south of Buenos Aires. His parents had immigrated to Argentina from New England to find a better climate for his father's health, which had been threatened by tuberculosis, and also to seek their fortune (Frederick 1972, 11). Hudson spent his very early childhood on their first estancia, after which the family moved to a larger house and landholding further south near Chascomús; after his mother died in 1859, the family moved back to the original estancia, which gradually became much reduced due to his father's failing fortunes (Martínez Estrada 2001, 31, 41). Following his father's death in 1868, Hudson seems to have taken to wandering across Argentina and perhaps travelled as far as Venezuela and the Guyanas, working as a hired hand and gaucho and collecting bird specimens, which he sent to museums in Buenos Aires, Washington DC, and London. Finally, in 1874, at the age of thirty-three, he left Argentina forever and immigrated to England, where he began his writing career and continued his work as a naturalist (Frederick 1972, 13-14).

Hudson's work falls into four main categories—fiction, autobiography, travel writing, and naturalist studies, usually in ornithology—though there is a high degree of overlap between the four genres. His purely autobiographical writings and most successful novels and short stories are all set in Latin America, while his naturalist studies and travel works, usually describing journeys through isolated rural areas either on horseback or on foot, take place in both Argentina and England. The principal focus of the present study is on his literary work, especially his novel *The Purple Land* (1885), originally titled T*he Purple Land that England Lost*. His other fiction includes *El Ombú* (1902), later republished as *Tales of the Pampas*, and *Green Mansions* (1904), which is set in the Venezuelan jungle. His autobiographical description of his childhood, *Far Away and Long Ago* (1918), written in Cornwall when he was in his seventies, and the memoirs of his adventures in southern Argentina during his twenties, *Idle Days in Patagonia* (1893), also stand out for their lyricism, especially in descriptions of the natural world, and complement his fiction in many ways. The two works that are most important in terms of his acceptance into the Argentine literary canon are *The Purple Land* and *Far Away and Long Ago*, both of which are considered classics in the land of his birth.

Hudson lived in poverty almost all his life, both in Argentina and England; it was only with the publication of the romance *Green Mansions*, when he was in his sixties, that he achieved some measure of popular recognition and financial success. However, he was a man who was most at home in the outdoors and who felt a keen sense of communion and oneness with Nature, a kind of instinctive pantheism that Leila Gómez, in her study *Iluminados y tránsfugos: Relatos de viajeros y ficciones nacionales en Argentina, Paraguay y Perú* [Visionaries and Defectors: Travellers' Accounts and National Fictions in Argentina, Paraguay, and Peru] (2009), identifies with the New England transcendentalists and contrasts with the materialist rationalism of Sarmiento (54). Amy Ronner, a biographer of Hudson, has also observed that

"Hudson was not content to write *about* Nature; he wished to be Nature" (6). In fact, despite his lack of formal education, Hudson eventually became one of the preeminent ornithologists of the Southern Cone in his time and was a founding member of the Royal Society for the Protection of Birds in London (Jurado 1971, 117-18). His family maintained ties with many of the settlers in his area, both *criollo* and immigrant, but his chief contact with English-speakers in Argentina was with the Irish, Welsh, and English who had come there to live; thus, when he left the country, he chose to move to England, with which he identified more closely than with the United States. Hudson abhorred cities and loathed Buenos Aires, where he fell victim to a typhus epidemic as an adolescent; his experience in Argentina was far removed from that of the sons and daughters of the upper middle-class British professionals who lived in the capital. He spoke Spanish fluently, though his education was in English, principally home-schooling with a variety of eccentric and largely ineffectual British tutors (Martínez Estrada 1951, 57-60). In short, he was Argentine-born, bilingual, familiar from childhood with gaucho ways, and imbued with a deep appreciation of the natural world of the Pampas: he was as deeply Argentine as he was British.

The Purple Land was Hudson's first major work of fiction and achieved some notice in London before it "fell into oblivion," as the author himself notes in the introduction to the second edition (v), though the book was later to achieve greater fame. The novel tells the story of Richard Lamb, a young Englishman who has eloped with and clandestinely married a young woman named Paquita, and takes refuge in Uruguay with her to escape her father's wrath and avoid prosecution for absconding with a minor. In need of work, Lamb leaves his wife in the care of her aunt in Montevideo and sets out with a letter of recommendation to "the Mayordomo of a distant cattle-breeding establishment" in the interior. The novel is set in the 1870s, at a time when the violence associated with the traditional rivalry between the Colorado and Blanco parties in Uruguay was beginning to subside. Lamb travels from estancia to estancia through the central and southern Uruguayan countryside, from the River Yí to the hills of the Cuchilla de las Ánimas, unable to find steady paying work but discovering the beauties of the countryside and the immensely hospitable, passionate, humorous, and eloquent mentality of its people, with whom he constantly interacts. As he works, rides, exchanges stories, drinks, womanizes, and even fights in a battle during his long journey back to Paquita in Montevideo, he gradually becomes increasingly attracted to the people he moves among, taking on a gaucho identity when needed and even living by the gaucho code. Although he meets several British settlers with whom he forms a friendship, he does not get along with the "Colony of English Gentlemen" of sheep farmers he encounters (55-71), whom he finds to be haughty, slothful, self-absorbed drunkards, with no interest whatsoever in the people of the country, and he quickly leaves them to their own devices. Moreover, as Ariana Huberman has noted in *Gauchos and Foreigners* (2011), her comparative study of three Rioplatense authors (Hudson, Benito Lynch, and Alberto Gerchunoff) with links to languages other than Spanish, "[His] national affiliation changes throughout the novel" (40). Although he originally laments that England never managed to incorporate Uruguay into its empire after its two thwarted invasions of the region in 1806 and 1807, he ends the novel with a paean to the country's independence and hopes it can evolve in greater harmony with nature and its laws, so that Uruguayans may be "nature's noblemen" upon "this Green Continent" (367-8).

One of the most intriguing aspects of the novel is the linguistic palimpsest that underlies it—and which is also noticeable in other works by Hudson, especially those with a large amount of dialogue among local people. Oddly enough, though Lamb's verbal exchanges with all the characters in the novel are completely fluent, there are several spelling mistakes in his Spanish, particularly in his use of written accents. This may not be surprising, however, since Hudson's sketchy schooling was all in English. Thus we find *capataz* spelled "capatas" (43) and unneeded written accents on the i of "Paquita" and the *a* of "Oriental" (an inhabitant of the eastern shore of the Uruguay River and a synonym for a Uruguayan), mistakes that are common among people with little experience in Spanish spelling, whether native-born or foreign, and which make sense phonetically. Of much greater interest, however, are the traces of Spanish that underlie the English and which seem to show up most during heated exchanges with the women he meets or the eloquent retellings of stories by gauchos. Often these passages sound as if they had been spoken in Spanish and then translated literally into English. The coquettish Cleta, for instance, tells him:

> Adieu, Sun, husband of the moon. . . . Adieu, sweet, sweet friend, buyer of side-saddles! They were all lies you told—I know, I know. You want a horse and side-saddle to carry off some girl to-night. Happy she! Now I must sit in the dark alone . . . until Antonio, the atrocious, comes to liberate me with his old iron key—ah, fool! (338-9)

Roberto Ignacio Díaz, in his study *Unhomely Rooms: Foreign Tongues and Spanish American Literature* (2002), points out that the Spanish influence is strongest of all in Lamb's translations of songs and poems, which he usually prefaces by saying that he can't do them justice and they are only approximate. Thus his translation of a gaucho ballad is underlain by "the shadow of a *décima*, one of the favorite stanzas of oral poetry in Spanish," a fact which doubtlessly spurred both Spanish translators of the novel to render it in that exact poetic form (139). Interestingly, Hudson's work was lionized in England during his later years for the freshness and lyricism of his writing, which was unburdened by the literary scaffolding of education in classic British and European literature and had a touch of Spanish eloquence. In his introduction to *Far Away and Long Ago*, John Galsworthy calls Hudson's writing "a tonic, a deep refreshing drink, with a strange and wonderful flavour. . . . As a simple narrator he is well-nigh unsurpassed; as a stylist he has few, if any living equals" (viii). Hudson's contemporary and friend Joseph Conrad, another writer who moved between languages, also remarked, "You may try for ever to learn how Hudson got his effects and you will never know. He writes down his words as the good God makes the green grass to grow" (quoted in Ronner 1989, 4).

Hudson's work, however appealing it may now seem to Latin American readers, did not become popular in Spanish until twenty years after his death. It was not the initial appeal of his fiction, or even of his autobiography or naturalist writing that brought him to the attention of readers in his home country. Rather, it was part of a conscious effort of Argentine intellectuals in the 1930s and 1940s to integrate the author into the national consciousness. By that time, Argentina was already proud to have distinguished figures such as the paleontologist and anthropologist Florentino Ameghino, the geologist and archeologist Francisco Moreno, and the zoologist Germán Burmeister in its scientific canon, and in 1934 the journalist Enrique Espinoza published an article titled "La reconquista de Hudson" in *La Nación* in Buenos Aires, in which he advocated bringing Hudson's work into the mainstream of Argentine culture, especially on account of the author's outstanding contributions to the country's zoology (Gómez 2009, 22). Hudson, whom H J Massingham later called "el gran primitivo" in the title of his contribution to an anthology of critical articles on Hudson's work that appeared in Buenos Aires in 1941, was a man who had spent most of his life in the wild, observing the natural world; he knew the pampas intimately, both as a gaucho and as a naturalist. Literary figures such as Jorge Luis Borges, in his article "Sobre *The Purple Land*" [On *The Purple Land*] (1941), Ezequiel Martínez Estrada in his detailed study *El mundo maravilloso de Guillermo Enrique Hudson* [The Marvellous World of W. H. Hudson] (1951), and others associated with the literary review *Sur*, celebrated Hudson's work as a part of a national literary legacy that integrated the scholarly with the *gauchesco*, incorporating the immigrant vision (that of a well-read and cultivated immigrant, that is) into Argentine letters, enriching the pastoral writings of the time with a vast knowledge of the fauna and flora of the region, and incorporating a cosmopolitan, multilingual aspect into the national canon. Both authors went so far as to rate Hudson's work, and especially *The Purple Land*, as a broader foundational portrait of the national consciousness than José Hernández's epic poem *Martín Fierro*, which is generally considered the seminal work of Argentine literature, but there also existed a slight tendency to see Hudson as an outsider and even associate him with the English travellers who wrote on Argentina in the nineteenth century, although he was born in the country (Díaz 2002, 129). Their purpose, however, was not simply to play the part of devil's advocate: it was to redefine the Argentine national tradition (*el nuestro*) in a more liberal, heterogeneous way, and thus move it away from the narrower, more homogeneous interpretation of *Martín Fierro* and the gaucho tradition favoured by writers such as Leopoldo Lugones, who viewed it as a specifically *criollo* creation that antedated and excluded the immigrant Argentina of later years (Huberman 2011, 18-19).

A proliferation of translations of Hudson's work—even of his novels and naturalist writings set in England—followed during the 1940s, and from that time since, W H Hudson—now known in the Southern Cone as Guillermo Enrique Hudson—was a part of the Argentine literary canon. His essential Argentineness, combined with his cosmopolitanism, was embraced by the critical establishment and, later, by Rioplatense readers themselves.

Pablo Urbanyi, who currently lives in Ottawa, is one of the most active writers of satirical fiction in Argentine literature. Since the appearance of his first collection of short stories, *Noche de revolucionarios* [Night of the Revolutionaries], in Buenos Aires in 1972, he has written a total of fourteen works—ten novels and four collections of short stories—two of which have been published in Ottawa and the rest in Buenos Aires. Urbanyi's work has achieved considerable acclaim in Argentina: it is regularly and enthusiastically reviewed in the Argentine press, and his novel, *Silver*, a satirical fantasy based on the memoirs of a preternaturally intelligent gorilla raised as a human being in California, was runner-up for the prestigious Planeta award in Argentina in 1993. Throughout his literary production, which has included portraits of drawing-room revolutionaries, bumbling detectives, obsessive academics, unscrupulous physicians, pathological philanthropists, fascistic entertainers, and other characters, Urbanyi has retained a remarkably consistent satirical style and ability to touch on basic societal and existential problems in a comical way. Within Argentine literature, his work is part of a long satirical tradition that began in the *gauchesca* era with authors such as Estanislao del Campo, and in the twentieth century has included Leopoldo Lugones, Leopoldo Marechal, and Julio Cortázar.

Urbanyi was born in Hungary in 1939 and lived there throughout World War II, during which time his father fought in the Hungarian resistance movement. After the war, the family wanted to emigrate and had a choice between Argentina, Australia, or Canada. His father, thinking that English would be difficult to learn, opted for Argentina, and in 1949 the family settled in Longchamps, a town in the pampas just south of Buenos Aires (not far from where Hudson grew up), where his father eventually set up a toy factory. Although he continued to speak Hungarian with his parents, Urbanyi has always felt himself to be thoroughly Argentinian. He has maintained his contacts with Hungary, however, and several of his works have been translated into Hungarian and published there.

Irony has always been part of Urbanyi's life. The Hungarian village where he was born was ceded to Czechoslovakia after the war, so his first years of schooling were in the Czech and Slovak languages. In Argentina, he became interested in literature and started writing stories in the sixth grade. The distinguished poet Roberto Juarroz, who was the librarian at his high school, encouraged him in his reading of a variety of authors, especially those from the French, Russian, and Argentine literary traditions (personal interview, 1996). He attended the University of Buenos Aires for five years, enrolling in medicine, psychology, and physics, but finally dropped out to get married and successively become a carpet salesman, wool merchant, travel agent, nightclub owner, and desultory writer of fiction. As his literary activity increased, he was drawn to the great writers of the satirical tradition, such as Swift, Gogol, Prévert, Grimmelshausen, and Hašek. Like many Argentines, he was also interested in science fiction, particularly in the novels of Olaf Stapleton, Philip Dick, and Ray Bradbury. Following his early successes as a writer, Urbanyi was hired as an editor for the cultural supplement of *La Opinión*, at the time the leading centre-left newspaper in Buenos Aires. After the military coup against Isabel Perón in 1976, however, the paper was placed under government control, and the following year Urbanyi and his family left for Canada, where they settled in Ottawa. Eventually, Urbanyi decided to forgo his journalism career and make a living teaching Spanish, while plunging ahead with his writing, undeterred by the isolation of working alone in his native language in Canada; with time, in fact, his relative detachment from his surroundings has in some ways left him freer to focus more intensively on his literary vocation (personal interview, 1996).

Urbanyi's early works in Argentina proved popular and were widely noticed. *Noche de revolucionarios* offered a mordant, comical portrait of various aspects of Argentine society in disintegration and established his talent for pinpointing humorous contradictions in human behaviour. *Un revólver para Mack* [A Revolver for Mack] (1974), a detective novel, simultaneously parodied and fulfilled the rules of the genre, while at the same time criticizing the corruption and egotism that were undermining Argentine society. Once in Canada, his writing continued to explore human foibles, sharpening the edge to his satire and broadening its setting to North America and beyond. *En ninguna parte* [*The Nowhere Idea*] (1980), is a sophisticated, humorous, satirical portrait of life in a Canadian university (in which the narrator is writing a doctoral thesis on the work of W H Hudson), while his two following collections of short stories concentrate specifically on the debunking of a certain unthinking and often ingenuous positivism that underlies popular culture north of the Río Grande. His novel *Silver* (1994), in which a young gorilla is bought in a market in Gabon by an American anthropologist and his British wife and taken back to California to be raised in the "enriched environment" of their home and used as the subject of their research, is at once philosophical, comic, and deeply moving. It is narrated by Silver himself to an Argentine filmmaker, who later transcribes it after Silver dies. *Puesta de sol*, set almost entirely in Argentina, deals with the birth of a young couple's first child, who is mentally and physically incapacitated by spina bifida. Urbanyi examines the couple's plight with a profoundly touching irony, while at the same time satirizing the cruelties and self-interest of the medical system, which hypocritically wants to "save" the hideously deformed child to perform experiments on it. Urbanyi has also written a work of science fiction, a satirical erotic novel, and two volumes of *El zoológico de Dios* [The Zoo of God] (2006, 2010), which follow the life of a child born in Slovakia during the late 1930s as he lives through World War II and then flees Europe and grows up in Argentina.

Urbanyi's novel *Una epopeya de nuestros tiempos* [An Epic of Our Times], published by Ediciones Catálogos en Buenos Aires in 2004, is perhaps his most profound critique of life in Canada, a mock epic that explores the alienation of exile within the sterilized, technocratic culture of supposedly "advanced" societies. The book describes forty-eight hours in the life of Ernesto, an Argentine immigrant to a futuristic Canada whose fondness for all things natural and spontaneous has led to his increasing isolation within the empty positivism of a monolithic society that has sanctified conformity and consumerism and transformed them into a secular faith. It is the tale of a multidimensional person within a bidimensional environment, a psycho-social situation reminiscent of the curious mathematical science-fiction novel *Flatland*, by Edwin Abbott (1884). Even at home, in the company of his media-obsessed children and materialistic wife, Ernesto has had to isolate himself from his family in a tiny room in the attic, his "cardboard tower," where he meditates, makes endless notes, and attempts to write, barricading himself within a denigrated, irrelevant world of books and words. As he moves relentlessly from one banal and officialistic encounter with the artificial, rigidly conventional market utopia to another, he contrasts his current life with memories of the pampas and barrios where he grew up in Argentina, where the organic flow of human life—and economic hardship—held sway. Like Richard Lamb in *The Purple Land*, Ernesto moves through a foreign society, trying to play by its rules and interact with its inhabitants on their terms, but he finds himself alienated and at odds with it, rather than won over by its alternative reality.

Eventually Ernesto himself becomes obsessed with the relentless precision of the automatized civilization that he inhabits, symbolized by the incredible standardization in the size of eggs: How have the technicians been able to calibrate the nation's hens so precisely? The issue takes on a metaphysical quality and becomes something of an existential quest for him: perhaps within it is hidden the secret of society's drive to material perfection. He takes his question to a bureaucrat, Tom Bigegghead, of the Canadian National Egg Commission, but is disappointed and repelled by the excruciatingly technical explanation and hackneyed philosophizing that he receives in response. The experience destroys what little ability he has left to function in this standardized dystopia, and after heedlessly killing a policeman, he returns home and (perhaps) commits suicide—or simply goes to sleep: we never find out which. The whole flattened trajectory and banality of Ernesto's quest (the novel is dedicated to Robert Musil, the Austrian author of T*he Man without Qualities*) is a profound and acidly parodic comment on both developed and developing societies, as well as on personal freedom and conformity.

Urbanyi's work has probably been better received in Argentina than Hudson's was in England, at least until the publication of *Green Mansions* in 1904, which propelled Hudson to an international prominence that Urbanyi has yet to achieve. Urbanyi returns to Argentina often and works with his publishers in the promotion and diffusion of his books, which have appeared with several major publishing firms, and his popularity and critical appreciation are remarkable for an author who has not lived in the country for almost fourty-five years. Urbanyi continues to devote himself to his writing and works exclusively in Spanish. He has not gone out of his way to make contact with more than a handful of Canadian and Quebec writers, though he does participate to some extent in the Latino-Canadian literary scene. In this respect, Urbanyi is hardly different from Hudson, who never expressed much interest in Spanish or Latin American literature, though he was fascinated by local story-telling and poetry. Urbanyi's work, however, has already attained access to translation: three of his novels have been translated into English, five into French, and two into Hungarian, and is respected and enjoyed by those who know it. He has also received many writing grants from Canadian agencies such as the Canada Council for the Arts and the departments of Multiculturalism and External Affairs, and his work has been published in literary reviews and anthologies in Canada and Latin America. He travels regularly to Europe, where he has given conferences in Spain, Germany, and particularly Hungary, his birthplace, with which he has maintained close linguistic and literary ties.

Will Urbanyi's work ever be accepted into the pantheon of Canadian letters as Hudson's was in Argentina? Several factors have made it difficult. Though he is probably the most widely translated Hispanic author in Canada, translation does not necessarily guarantee access to the general reading public: reviewers are often reluctant to cover the work of someone who has difficulty in being interviewed or performing readings in English or French. At the same time, Latino-Canadian writers who work fluently in English, such as the Argentine essayist Alberto Manguel, or in French, like the prolific Brazilian novelist Sergio Kokis, have been quickly well received. Moreover, in contrast to Hudson, whose fiction set in Latin America appealed to readers there because of his deep roots and knowledge of the region of his birth, Urbanyi's satirical, ironic touch, with its undercurrent of deep and sometimes wrenching emotion and alienation, is somewhat of an anomaly in Canadian literature, and reviews—and sometimes even publication—have been difficult to come by. There is, however, a strong current of satirical fiction and intense irony in both English Canadian and Quebec literature, as the works of Earle Birney, Margaret Atwood, Réjean Ducharme, and Marie-Claire Blais attest, and it may only be a matter of time—and increased translation and exposure—till Urbanyi's work achieves greater acceptance. Moreover, Hudson's fiction was essentially about the land he grew up in, but from which he had emigrated. Urbanyi has chosen—in contrast to many Latino-Canadian writers, who prefer to continue writing about their homelands—to set a large part of his work in Canada and try to understand the culture of the land to which he has immigrated. He has observed that he will never be able to truly gain access to the Canadian mind and think like someone who has been raised in Canada (personal conversation, 2011). His fiction has not yet achieved in Canada the appeal of Hudson's in Britain, but Hudson's work only attained its canonical status some twenty years after his death. Just as Hudson, an English-speaking native son of Argentina, brought Argentines a new way of looking at their landscape and culture, Urbanyi, an adoptive writer of Canada, may succeed in convincing a Canadian readership to look at itself as humorously and self-critically as his works do. If so, Canadians will rediscover themselves in his fiction, just as Argentines have done in that of Hudson.

ANDREW MOODIE

Racial Re/Profiling: The Plays of Andrew Moodie

Leslie Sanders

> [B]lackness is surprising because it should not be here, was not here before, was always here, is only momentarily here, was always over there (beyond Canada, for example). This means, then, that Black people in Canada are also presumed surprises because they are "not here" and "here" simultaneously: they are, like Blackness, unexpected, shocking, concealed in a landscape of systemic Blacklessness; and, they exist in a landscape of Blacklessness and have "astonishingly" rich lives, which contradict the essential Black subject, In Canada, Blackness and Black people are altogether deniable *and* evidence of prior codes of representation that have identified Blackness/difference as irrelevant. (McKittrick, *Demonic Grounds*)

> Black Canadian theatre is centrally concerned with piecing together all of the ways in which diasporic expressions of Blackness can fashion a commentary on nationally local and global conditions...What these plays do is destabilize dramatically the mythical narratives of home, nation and citizen. From the point of view of the dispossessed, the subaltern, these plays are intended to do something...to represent the world from a vantage point from which justice and the ethical might be approached. (Rinaldo Walcott, *Dramatic Instabilities*)

The surprise of Black Canada, as McKittrick terms it, is its presence, to say nothing of its 'astonishingly' rich life," unimagined in the Canadian national mythology. That mythology posits two founding Nations, First Nations, and a multiculturalism that renders all other bodies Other, and from elsewhere. "Nation building," Eva Mackey argues in *The House of Difference: Cultural Politics and National Identity in Canada*, "is a dual process, entailing the management of population and the creation of national identity...Nationalism...depends upon mythological narratives of unified nation moving progressively through time," the narrative an account of how the nation's values of "fairness" and "justice" came to be (Mackey 23). In the Canadian narrative, the normative is white; that is, "Canadian Canadians" are understood to be white, and the social values espoused by the nation understood as the evolution of a "white" cultural legacy. Multiculturalism, now approximately a half-century l*eitmotif* of the national mythology, as well as national policy, assigns a place for those Others and creates a circumscribed narrative of belonging to a nation whose normative is white.

Perhaps for that reason, African Canadian writers and dramatists, whether born elsewhere or of multigenerational presence in Canada, particularly insist on claiming and inhabiting space and express "a dynamic interest in how geography is made and lived, through and beyond practices of domination" (McKittrick 92). Setting often is poignant in their works, whether fictional, poetic, or dramatic; that is, a central concern is a presence, and the claim, of Black bodies to their setting. In theatre, one might cite Djanet Sears's *Adventures of a Black Girl in Search of God*, inspired by the renaming of Holland Township's historic Negro Creek Road to Moggie Road after a white settler; George Elliott Clarke's dramatic version of *Whylah Falls*, set in rural Nova Scotia; George Boyd's *Consecrated Ground*, concerning the destruction of the historic Black community of Africville; Trey Anthony's *'da Kink in my hair*, set in a beauty parlour on Eglinton Avenue (Toronto denizens would know exactly where). All insist that what African diasporic communities would understand as a homeplace also locates itself in Canada.

This is not to say that Black bodies are not part of the national mythology. Prominent in Canada's self-narration is the Underground Railroad, Canadian shores as the place of refuge for those enslaved in the United States. Its history of slavery continues to be unacknowledged, however, and there is little record or understanding of over a century of postabolition Black immigration to various locations in Canada, particularly from the Caribbean and the United States. In schools, Black History (typically confined to February) concerns the Underground Railroad and the American Civil Rights Movement: students still are more likely to hear of Rosa Parks than of Viola Desmond, who was arrested for refusing to sit in the segregated section of a New Glasgow Nova Scotia movie house in 1946. The clear implication is that the freedom struggles that occurred south of the border were unnecessary in benevolent Canada.

This understanding of Black life and history as American is a matter of figurative as well as literal representation. What George Elliott Clarke resists in his essay, "Contesting a Model Blackness," on Walter Borden's *Tightrope Time*, and what André Alexis terms "borrowed Blackness" in his call for Black literature that takes up the specificity of the African Canadian experience, is the massive, even global, imprint of African American culture. Its images, particularly those drawn from cinema and popular culture, define and overdetermine Blackness, most particularly male Blackness, in the Canadian national imaginary.

Over approximately a decade, from 1995 to 2009, Andrew Moodie produced a body of plays that sought to situate specifically Canadian Black life in Canadian space and to counter that "model" or "borrowed" Blackness. Rinaldo Walcott and Idil Abdillahi recalled this period as a time when Canada was Black, marked by an outpouring of Black expressive arts, film, music, literature, visual arts and theatre (12), and Moodie had more plays on stage than any other Canadian playwright. His first play, *Riot*, premiered at Factory Lab Theatre, Toronto, in 1995, and was a smash hit. In some respects, *Riot* responded directly to André Alexis's querulous charge, for it addressed the complex relation of both events and images from the United States, and the intricate and heterogeneous nature of African Canadian communities with the nation.

All but one of the characters in *Riot* share a rented house in Toronto: Halifax-born Wendle, Ottawa-born Alex, who had been involved with Effie but has just come out, Vancouver-born Effie, Jamaican-born and Montreal-raised Grace and her nephew Kirk, whom she has recently brought up from Jamaica and who is on probation. Grace's boyfriend Henry, from Uganda, a businessman, is the final character. Not only the characters' origins, but also the conversations about Canada that rage through the household display a range of attitudes: towards national politics (the play opens with a debate on Quebec as a distinct society); regarding experiences of racism, from racial profiling to physical attacks; concerning how different viewpoints are affected by class (Alex comes from a wealthy background, others from far less privileged); about strategies of racial struggle; and over the outcome of the trial of the policemen who brutalized Rodney King.

The riot of the title is two-fold: in Act One, the characters watch the CNN broadcast of the acquittal of the policemen who beat Rodney King, and in Act Two the subsequent riots in Los Angeles; in Act Three a riot rages on Yonge Street in Toronto, after a rally protesting recent deadly clashes with Toronto police, particularly two in which young Black men were murdered by them in the course of an arrest. In the house, conflict arises when Effie spots a gun in Kirk's backpack, and again when he returns from the Yonge Street riot with a video camera. Kirk protests that the gun was given to him to hold, and the video camera, similarly, was thrust at him by someone in the mob. When he learns Alex, who had befriended him, is gay, he turns on him, flees and later calls Grace from Buffalo, where he plans to remain. Nothing finally is resolved in *Riot*; however, the play's succinct yet dense sounding of a host of issues, contextualized by historical events in the two nations, was resonant. The play closes with a desolate Grace, and Alex's recollection of his childhood desire physically to embrace the nation, lying on the grass hugging Canada and feeling hugged in return. "I miss that feeling. I really do," he concludes, then notices that they all had made it on to CNN.

Several aspects of *Riot* will also mark Moodie's later work. The first is his characters' deep knowledge of Canadian history and politics, and their firmly held opinions on matters not directly related to race and racism but rather to the course of the nation. The second is their command of technology: Alex, at least, is conversant with the inner workings of a computer, and Grace has lost an essay to a glitch in WordPerfect as the play opens. This ease with and knowledge of technology roots his characters firmly in the contemporary, in contrast to the historical or backward gaze of many African Canadian plays. His single historical play to date, *The Real McCoy*, focuses on a man whose contribution to a central engine of the modern, the steam engine, was critical. Third, his characters voice divergent views on social issues, in the manner of a problem play, not resolving them but rather rehearsing and enacting the debates. And finally, difficult conversations about sex and sexuality are part of the plays' fabric.

While immediate history gave resonance to *Riot*'s title, another aspect of the contemporary also provided a counterpoint to the play's dialogue with America. *Riot*'s setting is not in "the hood," the genre of film then at the height of popularity in the United States, and emulated, with a difference, by Canada's first "hood" movie, of the same year as *Riot*, Clement Virgo's *Rude*. Kirk's gun rocks the household community, and how or why he acquired it is never cleared up. A decade before what the Toronto media termed "the year of the gun," and in a city with a relatively low murder rate, gun violence among Black youth was just beginning to surface as an issue. More dangerous than any reality, however, arguably, at least, was the influence of the hood film on how the guns in the hands of Black youth were read, perhaps signaled in Moodie's play by Kirk's retreat to Buffalo.

If the genre was not on Moodie's mind to begin with, its popularity certainly gave rise to an incident that disturbed him greatly. He was approached by Al Waxman, an iconic Canadian actor and producer, to turn *Riot* into a film. They set to work, but draft after draft fell short of Waxman's vision. Finally what became clear was that Waxman saw Kirk as the play's centre; Waxman's *Riot* was a hood film and not the exploration of African Canadian life that Moodie envisioned. He quit. In his article describing his relationship with Waxman he recalled:

> When I wrote the play, I relished displaying the lives of Black Canadians. It's something we rarely see. All of our visions of Black North Americans are from south of the border. I think it's safe to say that most of us know more about boys living in the 'hood in South Central LA than boys living in the 'burbs of Etobicoke. In my career as an actor, I have been asked to play a pimp, a dealer, a crack addict, a gang leader and a Jamaican Rasta. All film roles. All for US film companies. In Riot, for the first time ever, I'm able to play a

> fast-witted university student from Ottawa, complete with a valley accent and a central-Canadian arrogance. I'm allowed to be Canadian. ("Too Canadian")

In Moodie's plays, it is being-Canadian that is itself surprising, in Katherine McKittrick's sense, and surprising, I would argue, to all members of his audience. Moodie signals the play's Canadian reality and the Canadianness of the characters by their knowledge of contemporary Canadian issues. His second play, *Oui*, a political romantic comedy set in 1995, opens with an Ottawa family battle over the upcoming Quebec referendum, playing the personal relationships between twins, their partners, and a friend against what might be termed Canada's unresolved familial struggle. His next work, *Wilbur County Blues*, invades that whitest of spaces, Ontario cottage country, and again, the setting is the foundational significance. When the refugee Ben Okigbo, who runs the local hardware store, adamantly refuses to let his son Gabriel attend a concert with neigbour Sherry's daughter Tabitha, Sherry asks him on a date so that the children can slip away. Ben and Sherry return to find his store vandalized. Fearing the attack is racial, he immediately packs his bags, but Gabriel refuses to move yet again. It is discovered that the store was trashed by a jealous suitor of Sherry's, and the play ends with two romantic couplings: Ben and Sherry, and two other characters—not Gabriel and Tabitha, who are simply friends. In this play, the racially motivated violence that all dread is not a factor, but Ben's burden of fear and sorrow has deeper roots. His wife, a journalist, had interviewed Ken Saro-Wiwa shortly before his arrest and execution, and for her outspoken work was seized and taken in front of her family, with Ben unable to save her. Ben's traumatic history reconfigures and broadens the local. *Wilbur County Blues* opens with a relatively innocent coupling, but darkens, first with apparently a racially motivated incident, and finally with a tragedy that occurred elsewhere but whose effect continues, despite a return to romance at the conclusion.

Moodie's next play, *A Common Man's Guide to Loving Women*, set in a newly acquired condo in downtown Toronto, with a wide balcony overlooking the city, concerns, as Rinaldo Walcott describes it, "the complicated lives of Black urban thirty-something males. (Or was it just urban males?)" (73). All four characters, friends, have good jobs; their banter, which occurs intermittently over computer games, ultimately concerns relationships with women. Robin is married; Chris, a lawyer, is dumped by his fiancé on the phone; as the play opens, Greg keeps trying to fix Chris up with a friend from work, with whom, the others insist, he is in love himself; and Wendle is about to lose everything because a woman from work he had been dating for six months, without sex, has, at the end of a romantic evening, charged him with rape. By his account, the sex was consensual until he had an allergic reaction to the condom, removed it, and continued despite the concern of his partner. Chris advises him to plead guilty, and in the ensuing arguments and discussions with all the characters, other complications are revealed: Robin reveals his brutal rape during childhood and is angry that his horrifying experiences and Wendle's behavior are equally termed rape. Moreover, we are told that in Wendle's case the woman's affidavit depicts the sex as brutal, and that he followed it with verbal violence, saying "all you white bitches are alike," and she further insists upon her determination not to become another Nicole Simpson—the cross-racial dynamic evoking the contemporary lightning rod for inflammatory judgment concerning interracial sexual relationships. The play concludes on Wendle's agreement to allow Chris, rather than the lawyer recommended by a male colleague, to handle his case. As Walcott comments in "Post OJ Black Men?" the play most centrally focuses on the crisis of heteromasculinity in the wake of feminism. All of the conversations, not only those over the central issue, struggle with the making of new relationships between men and women. Critical to my arguments regarding Moodie's work is that despite the allusion to the OJ Simpson case, racism is not the play's central concern. Ironically, as Chris reveals to his friends, he had had to sue his law firm because, for racial reasons, they attempted to break his contract right after hiring him. The case was settled by creating a department for him that turned him into the firm's Equity expert—a place he soon realized was the most important in the firm. By implication, African Canadian struggles for justice impact the advancement of society at large.

Balancing his attention to men, Moodie's next play concerns women. *The Lady Smith* locates itself "around Bathurst and Bloor" in Toronto, for at least a century considered the centre of the city's initially small and later rapidly expanded Black community. "It's a corner charged with the kind of keeping on that mixes luck and hope and resignation with the way things are going to be if you're Black in this city. And then again there's a whole lot of virtuosity in just getting over (36)," Dionne Brand concludes her essay "Bathurst," in which she memorializes the ways in which the subway station and neighbourhood became the location of political activism in the 1970s, especially for the Caribbean immigrants who had flocked to the city. As the play opens, Sylvia has just rented a room in the apartment shared by Holly and Cindy. She has just stepped away from her home and marriage; Cindy is about to get married to her girlfriend; Holly is having an affair with Jordan, a married man (who turns out to be Sylvia's husband), and is getting ready for a romantic weekend in Montreal. Girded by that central dramatic irony, the play explores love, marriage, sex, and friendship. Again, computers figure in the action: Jordan is a computer engineer, Holly, a graphic artist who is preparing a portfolio for job interviews. Sylvia destroys her romantic getaway by introducing a virus into Holly's computer. Yet for all its devices, the play's tone, and denouement, its ethical discussions, and its normalizing of gay marriage with the context of a larger Black community are important interventions into age-old and contemporary social realities.

These plays, all produced between 1995 and 2000 at major and well established alternative Canadian venues, were followed by *The Real McCoy*, Moodie's first venture into history. Learning by chance that the phrase "the real McCoy" referred not to the famous feuding families, but rather to an invention by Elijah McCoy, born in Colchester, Ontario, in 1844, his parents having made their way to Canada on the underground railroad, Moodie was intrigued at his absence from Canadian history. One version of the origin of the phrase "the real McCoy" is that, indeed, that it refers to McCoy's invention of an oil cup that made it possible for locomotives to operate continuously, rather than stopping to lubricate every ten miles. The excellence of his product over other versions led engineers to insist on purchasing "the real McCoy."

In Moodie's version of McCoy's story, motherless Elijah is brilliant and from childhood is obsessed with the laws of entropy. Educated as an engineer in Edinburgh, Elijah moves to Michigan to take a job obtained for him by his professor. However, he is relegated to stoking and oiling engines because of his race. On his own time, he invents the lubricating cup, to the incredulity of his employers, and ends up in uneasy partnership with them. Throughout his life racism continues to constrain his possibilities, but his restless and obsessively inventive mind is unconstrained—the ironing board, the garden sprinkler, treaded soles on rubber boots number among his fifty-seven patents. He loses two wives, the first to tuberculosis and his second in a car accident, and he dies raving (the historical Elijah McCoy did, indeed, die in an asylum, penniless and suffering from dementia).

In his "Playwright's Notes" Moodie writes: "The play is intended to be an allegory, or rather, a parable. The theme of which is our struggle with the fundamental entropic nature of the universe (vii)." For his parable, he created a play that moves seamlessly through short, evocative encounters, his six actors playing multiple roles, moving effortlessly among them. Holding the scenes together is both narrative and Elijah's obsession: "All systems, left on their own, tend to become disordered, dispersed, and corrupted," the adult McCoy observes just after his mother has died giving birth to him. "Everything whether living or not, wears out, deteriorates, decays, disintegrates, and is destroyed. Entropy. The supreme metaphysical law of the entire universe (10)." As he speaks, he tries to touch his mother, but can't. She, as does each character who dies in the play, has washed her face in a white bowl full of water. She picks up the bowl, glances at him and leaves. A harmonica has played a single note, which the actors hum. At his final words, the next scene begins.

In an argument with his employers, who don't want people to know a Black man is responsible for the invention that is making them all wealthy, Elijah asks, "Has it ever occurred to you, that all the evils in this country, the hatred, and ignorance, bitterness and greed are inefficiencies that corrode the gears of our society, and if it were not for this, we could truly be the greatest nation the earth has ever seen? (79-80)" Believing firmly in a rational universe, and that problems have solutions, life's blows drive him further into his mental battle with the universe, which he articulates as a struggle with God. Moodie's *The Real McCoy* constructs a man of immense stature, whose intense inner life fills the stage, and whose unremitting faith in Enlightenment principles draws him into madness. In recuperating Elijah McCoy, Moodie finds a correlative for the portrait of Black masculinity he has been investigating: deeply engaged in figuring out the world, larger than the constraints of a racist society, while never denying the pain of racism. "Anger closes your eyes. When you get angry, you can't see. Keep your eyes open . . . (13)," McCoy's father advises him.

Moodie's most recent play, *Toronto the Good*, comprises a very different intervention into race and nation. It returns to the problem play, seeking to expose and provoke issues facing Toronto. The play's title is an old soubriquet stemming from the city's nineteenth-century reputation as a bastion of Victorian morality. In claiming it as his title, Moodie effects what has become his characteristic claiming of Canadian space, and in the naming of many of his characters, he embeds Canadian history into the play as well. For example, the accused is named after Solomon Moseby, a runaway slave who made it to Niagara in 1837, was jailed for stealing his master's horse, and then escaped with the assistance of the local community. He fled to England, where he became free, and later returned to settle in Niagara. Solomon's sister is named Rose Fortune, after the first female police officer in North America, a child of Black Loyalists. Elsie MacGill, the chief aeronautical engineer at Canada Car & Foundry, was Canada's "Rosie the Riveter."

Both in his Playwright's Notes for the published version of the play and in a video interview with TorontoStage.com, Moodie details his extensive research and the interviews on which his dialogue is based. The writing, he says in his Notes, was "like lancing a boil." He claims no message, but rather that the play comprises an investigation into the gun violence, principally among young Black males, that still plagues Toronto. In the interview, Moodie says that it is incomprehensible to him, and questions the mindset that engages in a gun battle in the middle of the city, killing a bystander. Racial profiling, however, is the umbrella issue and the principal conflict, as well as resonant trope, for the play.

As in *The Real McCoy*, Moodie works with short vignettes, his actors playing multiple roles, at times providing a chorus or a character addressing the audience. In the opening scene, Thomas, a crown attorney, is stopped by the police while biking to a store. He comments to the audience: "And then the incredulity starts to spark and becomes a kind of smouldering rage that . . . actually, well . . . there are two things happening at the same time: the rage and the fear. The fear that your rage is going to get out of control and make the situation worse" (8). In the next scene, however, he meets the police officer, who has been accused of racial profiling Thomas, on whose testimony his prosecution rests. Officer MacGill, a white woman from Nova Scotia, claims in her testimony not to "see colour," saying that she would enter her high school through the door used by the Black students, and her father was one of the few doctors who accepted Black patients. Her version of the arrest in question is that the defendant was driving "erratically," and when she stopped him, she discovered a gun. Simon, the defense attorney, denies the erratic driving and terms the case is based clearly on racial profiling.

We first encounter Solomon at his interview with Simon; he is silent until he is asked if he has questions. "I need a job," he responds. "You know where I can get a job?" (48). When next we hear from him, a few scenes later, he holds a microphone and raps his story: "Fa REAL. This is me, Solomon Moseby, . . . I'm gonna break this down for y'all. So y'all can bear witness . . . Lord only knows you never wanna be this. / I got no voice and yet I must scream this / I've got a soul, but y'all just look through me . . . "(68-9). The rap ends with a gun battle as the chorus calls out the names of young Black men recently killed by police in Toronto with the refrain "We bear witness." Solomon fires and is multiply shot in return. As the Act ends, the outline of his body remains on the stage.

Other characters from the underclass are also drawn in outline. Thomas's Franco-Ontarian wife Almanda teaches school and has particular difficulty trying to help Violet, whom she thinks is brilliant, but who hands in no work, and is disrespectful. When finally she demands Violet simply write one poem for the year's work, Violet complies. Amanda reads it while waiting for her ultrasound. It is spoken by Violet: "My life is like a roller coaster. Everything seems to go wrong . . . He said he would shoot my family. If I did not say yes. Sometimes I feel like I'm not supposed to be around . . ." Later a youth appears at her classroom door to say Violet will not be returning because her yard was shot up, and she and her mother had to move, but that she is grateful that Amanda tried to help. The hopelessness of poverty, the willful failure of government and authorities to address social issues, the deep pain and anger of a community unable to see a way out, all are powerfully suggested in the play, but with relatively few words, and little character development. Despite Solomon's rap, he remains a cipher, like an outline left on the stage. Violet, too, says little, as does Solomon's sister Rose.

Moodie puts the progressive analysis of Black poverty and violence into the mouth of Simon, the defense attorney, a white member of the NDP; it is Thomas who espouses the conservative position that everyone has choices. He gives an interview to Mary Ann Shadd, a journalist; her article lambasts him for his inability to understand the pressures on the poor. Yet race binds Thomas to the community: his final questioning of Officer MacGill turns vicious; and he attempts to force her to plead guilty in return for Solomon's naming of his shooter, who is wanted by the RCMP. The sole support of an ill father, she refuses and demands a trial. Only Solomon's agonizing death, movingly described in his voice, allows the play's complications to resolve, but the various personal resolutions that conclude the action are only that. The police are off the hook; Rose has lost her brother; Thomas seems to have learned nothing. Moodie told reviewer Pamella Baily, "I want to start a dialogue, a real, substantive dialogue that can include citizens and policy makers. I don't believe that theatre can change the world, but I believe that a play can create a conversation that resonates within a community, and that community can create change, if they choose to. If *we* choose to" (Review).

Clearly, *Toronto the Good* sought to implicate, and so provoke, Canadian society at all levels, to consider its various responsibilities for racism, social neglect, and the "othering" of the poor, whose lives it does not know or understand, but whose desperation leads to murderous violence. That is, the play indicts on the grounds of class as well as race. Thomas has little understanding of or sympathy for the social issues confronting Solomon and the world from which he emerges. Yet he, too, is endangered by racial profiling, as the opening moments of the play make clear. That shared danger does not, however, translate into "community." Almanda, in her caring for Violet, and Simon in his defense of Solomon and in his politics comprise the principal voices of human concern, although neither are without fault in other regards. While *Toronto the Good* is powerful and eloquent in other respects, this timeworn strategy undermines, I suggest, what has been one of the strengths of Moodie's dramatic oeuvre: insisting on the completeness of the world Black characters create in Canadian space.

Moodie's focus, in all his plays, is on African Canadian characters who are not abject, who are not mired in poverty and hopelessness, but rather who are relatively socially and economically secure, interested in and conversant with a range of political issues, and successful in overcoming racial barriers. This focus is unusual, and significant, or, in McKittrick's terms "surprising." Moodie's characters represent not a possibility, but rather, actuality, an actuality hidden from the nation to which they lay claim and which does not recognize their existence. As a body of work, the plays comprise, I would argue, an experiment: can the universal, or even the normative, be represented, explored, enacted by Black bodies? Can, in Walcott's terms, "justice and the ethical" be approached through them? The question itself is a claim to place and a challenge to the nation, one the nation has not taken up.

This paper has focused on plays that have received a full production. Production information: *Riot*, Factory Theatre, Toronto, October 1995; *Oui*, Factory Theatre, Toronto, January 1998; *Wilbur County Blues*, Blyth Festival, 1998; *A Common Man's Guide to Loving Women*, Ottawa, National Arts Centre, March 1999 (with the Canadian Stage Company, Toronto); *The Lady Smith*, Toronto, Theatre Passe Muraille, March 2000; *The Real McCoy*, Toronto, Factory Theatre, February 2006; *Toronto the Good*, Toronto, Factory Theatre, January 2009.

DANNABANG KUWABONG

Dannabang Kuwabong's *Caribbean Blues & Love's Genealogy* and *Voices from Kibuli Country*

Horace I Goddard

In African and Afro-Caribbean literatures in English, writers continue to search for voices that express their legitimate concerns about their people on the continent and the Diaspora. Dannabang Kuwabong has written two collections of poetry which chart an unusual path to remembering the ancestral past: *Caribbean Blues & Love's Genealogy* (2008) and *Voices from Kibuli Country* (2013). The poems in these collections are mainly set in the Caribbean and in Hamilton, Ontario. Kuwabong's poetic journey is a reversed process in the historical retracing and discovery of ancestral memory. Normally, Black writers from the Diaspora seek their ancestral beginnings in Africa, but in these collections, the poet tries to unravel the skeins of ancestral memories embedded in the Caribbean landscape, culture, languages, and psyche. Memories are evidenced in dances, worship, forms of ritual, food, and song.

Kuwabong's poetic vision in his journey of self-discovery uses ancestral memory to uproot and present the ancestral past in the Caribbean. Kuwabong is a Ghanaian Canadian who was born in the Upper Western region of Ghana. Of Dagaaba ancestry, he received his education in Ghana, Scotland, and Canada and is currently a professor of Caribbean Literature at the University of Puerto Rico. He resides in Hamilton, Ontario. The first collection, *Caribbean Blues and Love's Genealogy*, is divided into two books. Book One begins with horror, hurt, and pain. "Wailing / wailing locked in the system" (1) is an attempt to break free from a muzzle "that blocks sound." The language in the preamble, "To My Caribbean Sisters," is rebellious, defiant, and creates an atmosphere of forgetfulness, but the poet persona intends to break open every calabash and gourd that locks up memories. This first poem identifies the poet with Caribbean peoples. He calls the women his sisters. He and they come from the same mould and hence a common ancestry. The poem opens with wailing which may be taken as an indication of loss. But this is not the case here, for wailing is a cry of discovery: "wailing birth at dark . . ." (3).

This poet's search for identity and meaning in the lives of the descendants of Africa within the Diaspora brings him a new awareness of his past. This knowledge, though rooted in pain, suffering and despair, knits together the historical connections of Blacks in the New World with their African ancestral past. This interest is similar to that of Edward Kamau Brathwaite, the Barbadian poet who lived in Ghana for many years unearthing his ancestry. "Child at Sea-Junctions," propels, what may be considered a lost past. The poet persona is persistent, irascible, and determined in his search:

> I come seeking
> Names for faces
> I come seeking
> Whispers from silences
> Meaning in madness (4)

The meaning of this search is more historic and religious than evidentiary and physical, after four hundred years. In "Child at Sea-Junctions," the poet declares:

> I am that child of leftover falcon feed
> I crawl from hidden bushes
> crossing by leaf on raging tides (4)

The "raging tides" bring to memory the dangers of crossing the Middle Passage during times of slavery. This is counterpointed by the declaration of his search for his origin:

> my beginning here is not of flesh

my beginning here is not of bone . . .
the song is gone
across a boiling sea
the memory rises from mountain tops to meet me
child of falcon feed
child of falcon feed
at the sea's junction (5)

One of the predominant images in this poem is that of the "falcon child." This image supports the earlier point about determination and persistence, for the falcon has keen vision, powerful wings, and swiftness of attack.

The image of the falcon prepares us for the poet's "Arriving in Nanny's Country: Jamaica." Kuwabong's journey parallels Derek Walcott's journey motif, albeit among the islands, while that of this poet begins in Ghana and moves through the islands of the Caribbean. The symbolic reference to the falcon echoes Yeats's use of the image in his poem, "The Second Coming." The second coming for this poet is truly the re-connection of the ancestors with their offspring in a spiritual way:

I smell my rebirth at dawn
beneath these ashes of blue mountain
I smell burnt flesh among ruins
I see the kambonse of Ashanti (7)

The evil committed by the kambonse of Ashanti in selling the poet's people, the Dagaaba, into slavery and their reappearance in Jamaica merge to form a single personalized identity crisis leading the poet persona to claim, "I am the foundation bone" (7). The persona descends from the people kidnapped by Ashanti warriors, referred to as the kambonse in Dagaare.

Thus, when he claims to be the foundation bone of Jamaica, his statement undermines the general claims of African Caribbean scholars that Ashanti people were the only ones that resisted the slave trade when in fact they were the main collaborators with the European enslavers in the evil enterprise (see Gates Jr, 1999; Kannkpeyeng, 2009, among other contemporary historians). The recognition of foods not known to be staples among Ashanti is telling. The persona details how the Ashanti slave raiders captured his maternal ancestors such as Namuuma and Dabarima, whose experiences are often elided in the history of the African Caribbean people. Ashanti warlords received guns from the Europeans and became powerful enough to conduct raids for capturing slaves from the Ashanti hinterland. When they could no longer obtain slaves from other ethnic groups, they sold their own people, including other Akan groups of which the Ashanti is a part. Thus, the persona's claim is existential and historical in "...this land of misty blues... / somewhere in these maroon caves / sunsets begin in nanny march" (7). The maroon caves reference the rock caves at Sankana that hid escaped captives in his part of Ghana (Kankpeyeng 2009). Their arrival in Jamaica is an existential reality. The rebirth of ancestral memory is made evident in the food. The fruits and vegetables—mango, tamarind, sorrell, ackee, and callaloo—are all food crops among the Dagaaba and other Northern Ghanaian groups taken and enslaved in the Caribbean. The poet shows his excitement at this reunion of kindred spirits when he disembarks from the plane and exults with joy in his "homecoming," for it is "vibrations of the occiput / looking, seeing, knowing / the curved rays to rebirth" (9).

Memory is ignited and even though the arrival in Jamaica is painful because of the pain of separation especially from Northern Ghana, and the long silence of history, "the whirlpool of memory begins" (11). Memory retraces the capture of the forefathers and foremothers, of brothers and sisters: "those chained to the rock above water/ only tongue prints remain/ in the taste of aleefu in ackee" (11). In the foods, in the faces of the people, there are "circling dreams of lost roots/ rising solitudes of newness" (12), reactivate what was presumed lost forever. I often say that the slaves did not come alone. They brought their memories, their culture, their languages, traditions, and customs and planted them in these new lands of the Caribbean. Although the poet persona is overwhelmed by history screaming out at him, there is joy in finding elements of Northwestern Ghana in Jamaica and a strong link with Ghana. Words seem inadequate representations; only the foods seem adequate to reconnect the "womb of memory" (13). With this satiation of first beginnings, the persona leaves for Barbados.

The Barbadian experience is not only barren but frustrating. The

African existence is overshadowed by the extant Arawaks. The memory of Africa is sterilized and is done, paradoxically, with seawater. Barbados emerges as a "rock of emptiness" (15), overshadowed by all things British—culture, symbols, nomenclature. The statue of Admiral Lord Nelson in the heart of the city underscores this point. The explanation for this is twofold. Barbados was a British colony from 1621 until its independence in 1966. It is sarcastically referred to as Little England by other Caribbean people. The British first settled the deforested island long after the Arawaks had left in the 1500s. Secondly, between 1627 and 1800, Ibos from the Bight of Biafra formed the majority of slaves shipped to Barbados. The foods, the historical-cultural vestiges on the island such as childbirth, festivities, and dances, all reflect the influences of the Igbos. Nevertheless, I concur with the poet that Albion overshadows the lives of Barbadians so that "here sea water lashes history away" (16) and the people are "chained to a desire to forget" (19).

The poet leaves Barbados disappointed and journeys to Guyana in search of ancestral connections. In Guyana, he plunges into the country. Water becomes an essential metaphor. It defines "the concourse of life"; it "defines the discourse of truth" (23). Georgetown is welcoming; it is alive with its water affiliations in dams and rivers. The smiles of Guyana are paved with "gold" (28); but this is a mere mirage, for Rodney dies "close to this brown water" (29). From the welcoming geography of Guyana, the traveler finds himself back home in downtown Hamilton. He yearns for a spiritual love connection with the Caribbean.

Book Two of this volume, "Love's Genealogy," takes on less of an urgent tone in the quest for vestigial, ancestral traits embedded in memory. He now returns to his Canadian home and maps its streets and their poetic significance. He is on firmer ground here. Hamilton has a large population of Ghanaians. Thomas Y Owusu, a Ghanaian social scientist, "reveals that Ghanaians have established a relatively large network of township, ethnic and national associations (www.thepatrioticvanguard.com/specialreport). The poet in the Hamilton poems uses romantic and sexual language, as to a lover. The city displays unrequited love, and "Mapping" reveals a sense of misdirection: "I fear I cannot retrace my own steps" (33). Memory seems obfuscated by the streets. The poet is disappointed in his cartographic attempts at mapping "terra nova" (35).

There is a subdued and reflective tone in these poems, with "dreams / dozing on notions of a return" (35) as the poet searches for memories that would "lead me to journeys of my beginnings" (37). Beginnings here are undefined. Are they related to the poet's Ghanaian origin or his search for ancestral connectivity in the New World? In any case, there is also a prevailing mood of despair within the silences in the Hamilton poems. It is as though love, ceasing to be real, takes on "memories of dreams" (38) that are fleeting.

In "Love's Genealogy," forgetfulness plagues the memory. Memory must start somewhere, either in historical facts or in empirical physical evidence. Memory must have a beginning and through a continuum lead to a point or place. However, the poet recognizes that there is stagnancy in his search for an elusive wholeness. He declares: "I at the start of nothing/ mere distractions of refractions" (40). Love and passion seem futile on this journey and the "way forward is but a memory" (41). His journey as a pilgrim on uncharted terrain, wandering through darkness, is reminiscent of all things that are transient memories. Genealogy becomes the "invisible tree" (49). Roots search for water so that life will continue. The search for the ancestral umbilical cord between Ghana and the the Caribbean disjoins slowly into "wounded dreams" (52). There is an unraveling of desire and passion in this second book. There is loneliness, a "mask of misery" (54) and a sense of anomie:

> Through a tongue no-one hears
> Warble my distress no-one hears
> Wink my deliriums no-one sees
> Tears of my dejections, no-one wipes (54)

The poet laments the effacing of history. It seems as though "no-one" cares, hears, or thinks about a past that is lost to Blacks. His longing and desire to reconnect to the ancestral past are thwarted by the indignant crowd. He pauses to reflect and declares:

> across Caribbean sea
> halfway on these mountain slopes
> I erect a checkpoint
> between my mind's freedom…

what vision of the heart I carry
lurks like a frightened frog
in wrinkled ideas of history (58)

Four hundred years of separation bring no concreteness to the poet's search. All is silence, lamentation, and inescapable pain. The past is buried "in the dark, humid dusk / the voices recede, recede" (59). Memory grows faint and only emptiness and despair remain. In the closing poem of the second book, there is a glimmer of hope in futile love as the poem longs for a relationship: "If only I could be yours/ I will be your terra nova" (63).

In Book Three, "Miscellaneous Adventures," the poet returns to his theme of despair, loss, and the failure of memory to recreate a remembered past that flows into the present. He admits that he is "not bitter / I only sorrow in my womb" (68). The sorrow emanates from his inability to hold on to the vestiges of his ancestors in the Caribbean. In "My Last Testament," he sets out the conditions for his entombment, these being according to burial rites in his homeland. He wants to be "draped in a spider-shaped shroud" (71). One may be tempted to rush to conclude that he is borrowing from Akan folklore as is often concluded when the spider is mentioned. The spider is central in Dagaaba mythology, folklore, and spirituality (Goody 1972) in Ghana, Burkina Faso, and Cote d'Ivoire. Yet these people had no cultural affiliation with the Akans. Indeed, Kuwabong 's *Naa Konga: a collection of Dagaaba Folktales* (1992), *Kyoore's Dagara Folk Tales* (2012), and other works testify to the ideological and cultural differences and similarities between the way the spider is presented in the savannah and the forest belts of Ghana (private communication with Kuwabong, 2019). Thus, the poet here is not referencing the Akan Ananse, but the Dagaaba Badare. Among them, he is also a trickster figure but does not go scot-free for his selfish tricks. When caught, he is disciplined, but never tires of trickery and selfishness. Among the Akans, he is hardly punished, which tells of how the two groups view the spider even if he or she is a culture hero among the two groups. The spider web is also used as the resonator membrane in the gourds that act as the loudspeakers for xylophone keys. Thus, he still wants to be able to continue to contribute to the culture of the people through music even when dead. The poet wants to spin his stories of the remembered past or have his work memorialized for future generations. That will be his legacy for posterity. The final link is symbolizes the biological connection between mother and child in which the umbilical cord of Diaspora Blacks will once again be connected to the poet's motherland, Dagao, that is, Africa.

"Love's Genealogy" is a fitting conclusion to the poet's journey of discovery and retracing ancestry. He has seen and heard enough about the African Diaspora in the Caribbean and the Americas. Kuwabong, like Brathwaite, searches for meaning to the deracination and dispossession of Blacks in the New World that is not captured in their language, lifestyle, or history. For him, his journey of discovery ends with hope. His interest in the cultural, spiritual, and other physical connections of New World Blacks to their African ancestral past will be the foundation of new beginnings. Kuwabong's worldview is framed by the themes of melancholia, identity, birth, death, isolation, loneliness, and displacement. The journey motif is linked to the poet's growth and craft as a poet and scholar.

Voices from Kibuli Country extends the discourse on the poet's search for the links between Ghana and Blacks in the Caribbean. In both collections, we see the persona searching for elements of history and memory to revive that connection. A great number of Ghanaians through slavery and current migration live in the Caribbean and the Americas. Hamilton, Ontario, Kuwabong's adopted hometown, is the nexus from which he branches out on his journeys. With Hamilton as his base, he can make comparisons and interrogate the dialectic of reality and memory. Thus, the travel motif creates dissonance between the desire to unearth historical evidence for the ancestral links and the reincarnation of the Ghanain "self" within the Caribbean.

Hamilton is an industrial city. Smog and physical decay tend to cover the landscape. The early poems in this collection spark the act of remembering and breaking out from darkness into knowing. The poet demonstrates a divided consciousness: one that knows that his ancestors' DNA is found in Caribbean people, and the other a consciousness that reflects life in Ghana before his departure. He remembers life as a soldier and a peacekeeper and his eventual escape from Ghana to freedom from death. Remembering is a tug-of-war between his search for ancestral traces and the reality of his exilic separation from his country of birth.

Helplessness and frustration in his search for connectivity between the past and the present create barriers that he must overcome. His move to Hamilton presents a sense of a new beginning in the poem "New Year's Eve": "To Hamilton then a steel city we came with hope" (5). Amid the joy of being free, fear lurks around every corner, and shadows of Christmas, which should bring peace and goodwill, instead present loneliness, isolation and longings for a simple "sip of Typhoo or a cappuccino / all that is gone now only the shadowy memories remain / they fade daily and with each cold winter night" (6). Memory is no longer liberating; rather, it is a prison and is painful. Shadows do not hide the pain of rejection and isolation; they become the covering for "stifled lamentations of rejected love" (18). The poem "Those Who Step into Shadows" points to death by suicide. Canada's rejection of the poet's love damns his life to one of blood trial. The shedding of blood is the symbol for the atonement for "the drag of ancient chains" (24). Images of the past are intricately bound up with the struggle to survive in this new land, this new geography. "In Dawn of My Dying 1," we see the past and present linked in a syncopated, incantatory dance:

> Where the drums have ceased . . .
> Syncopation now a monotone
> Only the echoes fade away
> Wavering over the wet goat skin (25)

The decline of the music indicates the falling off of love. The final lines of this poem strike a echo of Derek Walcott's poem "Far Cry from Africa," in which he laments the pain and anguish occasioned by his mixed-race origin of European and Black:

> I who am poisoned with the blood of both,
> Where shall I turn, divided to the vein?
> I who have cursed
> The drunken officer of British rule, how choose
> Between this Africa and the English tongue I love?
> Betray them both, or give back what they give?
> How can I face such slaughter and be cool?

> How can I turn from Africa and live? (Walcott 6)

The issue for Kuwabong is not that of his race but the love for his native land and Hamilton his adopted home: "I who am stranded here between teardrops and screams / Sweet darkness engulfing my hot heart of pain" (25). This pull between these two locations creates an unbridgeable gulf. Like Walcott's, the Kuwabong's mythology is woven into the fabric of his search for self.

"Massacre," the second section of *Voices from Kibuli Country*, continues the themes of isolation, pain, anger, and love. The introductory poems in this section are "While Listening to Kwame Dawes Speak of Healing Poetry—Day 1" and "Day 2: Listening to Kwame Dawes Speak about His interview with a Woman in Haiti." The poet surfaces the layers of pain and suffering confronting migrants/immigrants. The poems also speak to his reality of isolation. He reminds us that any outward or inward journey is marred by striving to connect two disparate selves. Using the form of a sonnet, the poet invokes world disasters such as Hurricane Katrina in Louisiana, the earthquake in Haiti, and the tsunami in Japan, all of which create death and sudden tombstones that temporarily erase memory. "After the Quake" and "After the Quake, Floods (Mami Cèléstè)" seem to be vodun reenactments of rituals for the dead:

> We each entered the prayer circle of ashes, emerging
> White lines covering our bodies and like skeletons, dancing
> We chant the litany of loas thanking them for receiving
> Those whose spirits had left so sudden at the earth's trembling
> (42)

The energy here flows with a circular motion and ignites the actions of the participants. Poetic references to the earthquake in Haiti highlight the lack of love among the people of the world. Many false promises were made. The help never reached the suffering masses that were dying from cholera. The poet mourns for Haiti and asks a poignant question, "Oh my Aiyiti! When again will my children laugh in innocent dreams?" (44).

The St Croix poems resurrect the memory of the ancestral past in the beat of the drums that bring "Ghosts of Taino and Dagaaba" (53), an obvious reference to the poet's ancestry. The "End-of-Year Performance Night" merges old-world and new-world customs: "The ancestors mingle with the descendants / The descendants mix with the invaders" (53). The Black rhythms break down barriers momentarily among the races, and all the people enjoy the music. In a subsurface way, the ritual dances and the drums seek to reconnect Blacks with their African ancestral gods. As the school children display their knowledge and pride in American English, a subtle and sinister thing is happening: the African child in the West is slowly losing his African consciousness through language, through economic, cultural, and historical European domination, deprivation, and absorption. The poet declares, "In this forest of Diaspora dreams / Memories are mangled and minced" (56).

The dance is the link between the people of St Croix and Ghana. This connection is historically accurate as the Danish Caribbean was hugely populated by people from present-day Ghana, the only part of West Africa where the Danes had any trading stations, with Christiansburg Castle in Osu, Accra as the biggest (Hansen 2002). The poet may also be recalling the drums to several uprisings in these islands, beginning with rebellion in St John in 1733 and the rebellion in St Croix under Buddhoe in 1848 that led to emancipation in the three islands. The drums sounded again in 1878 when, led by four women, a rebellion arose and many plantations were burnt to the ground. The poet laments that American cultural imperialism is erasing all this proud history. Yet, he is hopeful. Their movements are duplicated and "Retrieved from cell memory/Resurrecting what had been buried . . . / Here they are living the dance of the Guinea coast" (57). The poem "Admiring a Private Collection in St Croix" revives the poet's frustration with the colonizers' pilfering of ancestral treasures and the denial of self-knowledge in "an island where much is forgotten or denied" (59). At the museum, Carib artifacts are exhibited but there is nothing about West Africans, and while Whites can easily retrace their ancestry, Black children are devoid of history and language to capture their memories. "There is no memory of the slave boy" (62) who raises the flag for emancipation. Denial of Black contributions to the development of countries that have predominantly Black populations displaces their humanity in the New World, so blatantly boasted about by their colonial masters. The poet responds with a mood that describes the situation aptly: "I have come because I want to be angry at history" (59).

In the St Martin/Maarten poems, the poet returns to his rant about "the tumult of painful desires" (70). Despair is punctuated at times with the hope that the children of Africa will triumph one day, and that over future generations death will not dominate and their contributions will be recognized. Kuwabong is realistic and considers that his search and his dreams may be illusory: "I must remember this to myself / these illusions of discovery / these new castles of escape . . ." (67). Even though the dreams may fade into the background of history, the salt, blood, sweat, and tears of the ancestors are indwelling and bring the hope of redemption for Blacks in the Diaspora:

> yet I do not despair in my dreams
> for in this tumult of painful desires
> echoes of deliverance tales may yet resound
> for the children of Sekou of Mali
> for the children of Kumbey of Ghana
> for the children of Gao of Songhai
> for the children of Manlarla of Dagao (70)

In this Judeo-Christian construct employed by Kuwabong, redemptive hope and new beginnings are envisioned. Clearly, as an ardent Catholic, the poet believes in the final victory of good over evil, of truth over falsity, and life over death found in Revelation:

> death expires in a white pool / of silence
> and the white horseman
> rallies daemons of justice
> rallies daemons of despair
> from the shadows of these archipelagos (Césaire) (71)

The white horseman is deceptively introduced to make us think it is the coming of Jesus as predicted by John in Revelation 19:11-21. However, this rider on the white horse references European conquerors, who will storm and pillage every corner of the world. The rider on the Black horse is the one that will come with the scale of justice and equitable sharing of resources. He will come to make sure the olive tree is not destroyed (6: 5-6). Thus it is the Black rider from whom justice will be meted out to those who are dead or are dwelling on the earth at His coming. As John says, because his voice will come from the living:

> And I looked, and behold, a white horse
> And he who sat on it had a bow; and a crown
> was given to him, and he went out conquering
> and to conquer. (6:2)

With the defeat of death and the promise of a new life for the righteous, there is renewed hope that Blacks will receive justice in this world or the next. Then one will be able to walk in ancestral footsteps:

> for we who perch on bayonet dreams
> have no more nightmares to offer
> only a sealed gourd of dread seeds
> that seek black soil among granite
> swinging among these cataracts
> of Africa, Europe, America
> these archipelagos of hope (Césaire) (72)

While the poet is hopeful about the future, he uses some stark images. Black soil represents fertility, but the soil overlays granite, which is impenetrable, and indicate the perpetual disconnect among the races.

His travels in the Commonwealth of Dominica raise more questions as to his identity and African connections. Two questions are asked: "I wonder who is Kibuli? / I wonder what is Kibuli?" (75). It is obvious that the poet is aware of Kibuli as a place in Uganda, but wonders about its significance in Dominica. Kibuli is one of the hills in Uganda's capital, Kampala. Kibuli, therefore, connects Uganda in East Africa, Ghana in West Africa, and the Commonwealth of Dominica in the Caribbean. Nationally and geographically all three are bound by historical ties of British colonization and the Trans-Atlantic slave trade under British maritime rule. Thus, the umbilicus binding them will not rot and fall off, neither will their physical and spiritual links with each other through Mother Africa be severed. The poet has great hope that one day these connections will be better manifested in the creativity and resilience of his people in Africa and the New World.

These two collections draw their inspirational language from English, Dagaare, Ghanaian Pidgin, and the Caribbean tongues and is informed by their intertwining histories, myths, and experiences. As soon as the poet kicks one in the gut of memory, he then reassures the reader that memory will create new beginnings for African peoples. The poems are intense, beautiful, and syncopating like the dances of the Guinea coast. I particularly like the drumbeat in these lines from "Shadows on Concession Street":

> blood is the trial!
> peace to the world
> blood is the trial!
> goodwill to all
> blood is the trial!!
> Who step into shadows
> Only blood is the trail! (17)

The rhythms are incantatory, like the calling of the "mwime" (deities) and ancestors in Dagaaba divination. Kuwabong's ear for Caribbean speech patterns is manifest in these lines: "so is walking I walking sofly sofly / is looking I looking new dreams (Kibuli, 62). The final poem, "Joan Fayer Kuori Yelbie," a tribute to Professor Jane Fayer of the University of Puerto Rico written upon her death, was sung by the poet in January 2018 at a poetry reading in Montreal. The dirge sung in his native language, Dagaaba, indicates that musical cadences of West Indian songs have their origins in West Africa. Overall, these collections reveal the poet's tremendous research into ancestral consciousness, historical relevance, myths, culture, language, and survival. They show that "the rediscovery of ancestral experience is intimately bound up in memory" (Goddard 37). In the West Indies, where Adam suffered amnesia, the past is fragmentary, but Kuwabong manages to capture elements that portray wholeness in his search for an ancestral past in the voices of English bards, the rhythms of Africa and the creolized language of the Caribbean and West Africa. This yoking of the past and present, infused with his deep sense of exile and the immigrant/emigrant's pain, make both collections erudite, memorable, and compelling.

M NOURBESE PHILIP

Haunting the Human: M NourbeSe Philip's Poetics of Un

Kate Siklosi

> I have for the longest while been interested in the power of the prefix un. Two letters that somehow are powerful enough to reverse certain acts or states, but that didn't work for others. The prefix un can be seen to be a kind of spell. (M NourbeSe Philip[1])

> So it is that boundary which interests me, between flesh and time, between what's sealed and what's open, between the words we speak and those that unspeak us. (Jorie Graham[2])

We know from feminist writers such as Audre Lorde and Hélène Cixous the power of recreation, revision, and rewriting in reestablishing agency for marginalized peoples within dominant scripts of being and belonging. But what if we began from a place of "un," or, *not*, as opposed to "re," or *again*? In other words, what new forms does the category of the human take on if we undo it, rather than redo it over again? To see the human as not becoming, but undone? What lies beneath; what came before what is? In other words, what is human, and what is the Unhuman? Such questions have haunted the poetic interrogations of Caribbean Canadian poet and activist M NourbeSe Philip throughout her poetic career. Under Philip's hand, the prefix "Un" becomes a tool for undoing the colonial project and its hold over narrative; however, in its refusal, and its desire for other worlds, it also opens a space of vibrant, kinetic, and generous connection to language and storytelling.[3]

In what follows, I put one of Philip's recent works, *The Book of Un with Undex* (2017), in conversation with two of her major previous works, *Zong!* (2008) and *She Tries Her Tongue, Her Silence Softly Breaks* (1989), to explore how her sustained poetics of Un from past to present creates a haunting, uneasy, necessary, and critical lens for human knowing, human telling, and human being.

Unbegin: *The Book of Un with Undex*

In the spring of 2017, Philip was mailed a 500-card Rolodex by a small American production house called Container and was asked to transform the object into a work of poetic art. She transformed the blank Rolodex—a portmanteau of the words rolling and index, a now archaic form of organization that has been replaced by digital data storage—into *The Book of Un with Undex*, a stunning work of poetic concrete art that turns outdated and mundane into the extraordinary using burnt paper, coffee, beet juice, tea, gold leaf gilding, and ink:

Figure 1. Image of *The Book of Un with Undex*, used with permission of the author.

The "Unrules for the Book of Un" included in the Undex asks the reader to "unbegin to unread" the textual object but warns, "Be ready to unenter the unlogical world of the Book of Un" (Philip, *The Book of*

Un with Undex, np). The *Book of Un*, the story told in the *Undex* object, takes the form of an origin story of the Unpeople who, before discovering the power of the Un, were largely a people that were confused with their history and their present. As Philip writes, "Death was all the time with the people as they loved and hated and hated some more, not knowing why they hated, or fought, or killed, or had wars" (np). All of this unknowing is happening while "Deep in the centre of time, the Story of Un slept on and on" (np). The Story of Un is a seeded, buried history that becomes fertilized by the tears of a crying girl. After being nourished by the tears, the seed "grows" and the Unpeople begin to remember an "unmemory of a time long ago, or the unfuture of a time uncome" (np). The seed eventually grows into a mighty untree, and the site becomes a meeting place where the Unpeople gather to untell their stories.

Under this spell of the Un, "the magical word with only two letters that could change anything that had happened, making like it never happened," (np) the Unpeople begin to remember this Time of Un, and their lives become a moving montage of successive events untold, undone, their present a series of unpasts.

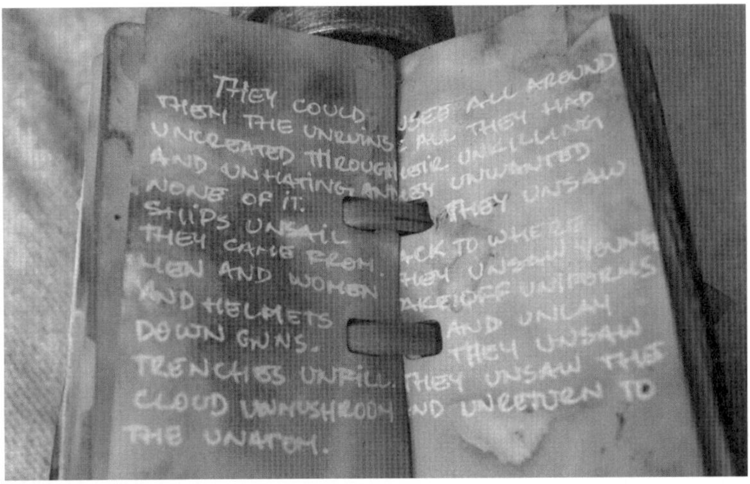

Figure 2. Pages from *The Book of Un with Undex*, used with permission of the author.

Moving backward through some of the catastrophic events of history, the Unpeople witness their history and that of the world in rewind. In this oscillating universe, time is out of joint: "They unsaw ships unsail . . . unsaw trenches unfill . . . unsaw the cloud unmushroom" (np).[4] As the Undex turns around its spindle, we can visualize these scenes almost cinematically in reverse, everything is restored to its unstate. Just by adding two letters to these words, Philip makes the disorientation and unlogic of her narrative strangely familiar and intuitive, yet uncannily so. As the worn pages of the *Undex* are turned around its spindle, the work reveals the magic of the prefix un as a sort of linguistic spell: as Philip says in the epigraph to this essay, "un . . . two letters that somehow are powerful enough to reverse certain acts or states, but that didn't work for others" ("M NourbeSe Philip"). The prefix *un* highlights language's relationality, its flux of meaning, and also its unreliability as an arbiter of being and nonbeing. Why, for instance, can we "unearth" something, or leave something "undone" but not "unpeople" or commit acts of "unwar"? When added to a word, the prefix un negates what that word signifies but leaves the word intact; it does not erase the word itself. In this way, the prefix becomes a haunting hinge that shadows words in a space of unbeing, one that asks us to get involved in the labour of the text, to feel out our responsibility to yearn for the unsaid and thereby produce meaning outside what has been told to us.

The Un occupies a spectral ontological and linguistic space between what has been said, what hasn't been said, and what remains to be said. This mode of unwriting is, for Philip as a woman Caribbean writer, an "unmanageable" act, since "the managers have not traditionally thought of us as thinkers, or writers, or keepers of memory and history" ("Managing the Unmanageable" 300). The subversion of grammar and language, then, is not only a resistant poetic praxis for Philip but necessary survival: "How does a writer who belongs to one of those traditionally managed groups begin to write from her place in a language that is not her own? How does she discover or uncover a place and language of empowerment?" (Philip, "Managing" 296). By manipulating—or by *refusing*—the function and order of the index/rolodex, Philip transforms it into a poetic object that makes concrete other existent ways of arranging texts, knowledge, history, bodies, and social orders of being. As she writes about the Unpeople, "Together, they unlanguaged their hearts and untongued their thoughts . . . Was the undark the same as light, they asked, and unlight the same as the dark? Could they unbe? Should they unneed each other? Some unblacked themselves; others unwhitened their skins":

Figure 3: Pages from *The Book of Un with Undex*, used with permission of the author.

At first thought, to "unlanguage" and "untongue" might be read as acts of silencing; however, in the world of the Unpeople, the ability to release their stories and bodies from entrenched colonial scripts that fix their nonbeing is a radical act of liberation and agency.

The Unpeople find themselves released into a world where the dominant, privileged sense of reality is no longer the one that dictates, circumscribes, or erases their knowledge and articulations of self and collective being. *In Freedom Time: The Poetics and Politics of Black Experimental Writing*, Anthony Reed argues that Philip's work in *Zong!* "synthesizes two roughly contemporaneous understandings of concreteness—involving idealized notions of words and [B]lack experience—to 'unsay' common-sense notions and reopen horizons of thought" (23). Similarly, In the *Book of Un with Undex*, Philip centres her story around those words that are not, as we know it in common sense, able to be "unned"—words like *unhistory*, *uncried*, *unjumped*, *unocean*. Below is a list from Philip's rough notes that came to form the alphabetized Undex:

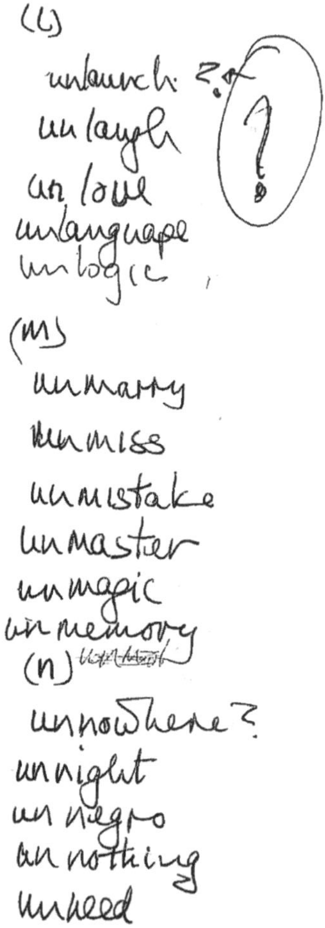
(L)
unlaunch ?
unlaugh
un love
unlanguage
unlogic
(m)
unmarry
unmiss
unmistake
unmaster
unmagic
unmemory
(n)
unnowhere ?
unnight
un negro
un nothing
unneed

Figure 4. M NourbeSe Philip's notes from *The Book of Un with Undex*. Used with the author's permission.

Adding un to the words we conceive of as already happening, or incapable of unhappening, like *unmaster*, and *unned*, establishes an undone poetics that undoes the Unpeople's history as it was told to them, and goes back to a time when such events were yet to be told.

The Unpeople, having harnessed the power of Un to uncover their stories and truths, "unbreathed their unhistory; they unswallowed the ocean and unfilled their lungs with briny water; they ungasped, uncried, and unjumped into the unwaters of the great Un of the unocean. They undrowned and unsank to the bottom of the unwaters and they were unfilled with unshame at what had unhappened to them" and "unlived happily unever unafter in the un of unbeing, unam, and unis" (np). Under Philip's hand, the Unpeople, a metonym for the people of the transatlantic slave trade, are poignantly made to unsuffer, to be unmurdered, unspoken for. Her manipulation of language crumbles the assumed concrete authenticity of historical narratives and unwrites the ordered rationalism and universalized humanism that attempts to singularize personal and collective experience and testimony. While we might associate absence with the prefix *un*, Philip undoes the negation instead of making it a transformative sign of agency and empowering presence.

We can think of the human, following the thought of Jamaican scholar Sylvia Wynter, as an atomic material, one that through stories and histories has a sedimented and striated composition that evolves with the winds and rains of eras and epochs. Wynter's work, like Philip's, is concerned with poetic "self-making" as resistance. Her work interrogates the category of "Man," how it has been reproduced over time, how it has been told to us using various epistemological frameworks that naturalize the category of Man versus that of Human. Wynter traces the ontology of "Man" back to the Big Bang, but she argues specifically that with European imperial expansion and colonial violence in the "New World," a specific kind of human—the western Man—became imposed as the universal norm for what Wynter calls the western world's "referent-we," or whom we mean when we say "human." When "Western Man" arrived in the "New World," his system of dividing the human by skin colour created various "types" and "genres of the human," which together play into a larger script of domination and subjection and continue to be readily ordered and classed in our present consciousness. As Wynter puts it, the European conception of Man "overrepresents itself as if it were the human itself" ("Unsettling" 260). Her work carefully breaks this totality open by tracing a shifting ontology of being as "demonic ground," a shimmering, vibrant plane where being is multitudinous and refracts as it comes into contact with untold material histories, presents, and futures. These refractions do not result in hierarchical "genres of the human" as the white supremacist narratives of the New World would have it, but rather, they reveal being as a complex relational landscape of multiple oppressions and multiple possibilities.

Poetry, for Wynter, is a viable means of articulating this shifting landscape, for she describes how poetic "acts of making," of deconstructing and then reconstructing, can "construct an alternative process of making ourselves human" (Wynter, "Ethno or Socio Poetics" 89). To unbegin to unread the category of human is to think critically of the epistemic violence in its wake, and to give voice to the human that haunts it. It is also a means of reconstructing social relations and identities, as the Unpeople's newly undone collective imaginary demonstrates. In this way, Philip's poetic object becomes a "field force which reinterprets and reinvents anew the meaning of the sign" (Wynter, "Ethno or Socio Poetics" 88). Like Wynter, Philip resists the singular imperial concept of humanity based on the Western ideal of the White Man. Her project, like Wynter's, is not to revision or redo the concept of Human, but to *undo* it: to go back to the bedrock and ask, first, "What does it mean to be Human"? Philip's project resists the presumed authority of a particular people to speak for and embody the truth of what *Human* means, has meant, and can mean. She poetically refracts the Human by bending its way of light with untold stories.

In short, Philip *haunts the Human* by meddling with its signs, its here-and-now, and undermining its surety with uncertainty in language and form. And in this way, Philip's work combines Wynter's desire for an Undoing of Western man's totalizing narrative with Jacques Derrida's reflections on the specters of history in *Specters of Marx* (1993). For Derrida, hauntology—a homophone of "ontology" in Derrida's native French—is a concept metaphor that calls attention to the very constructed, and shifting, nature of being. According to Derrida, "To haunt does not mean to be present, and it is necessary to introduce haunting into the very construction of a concept. Of every concept, beginning with the concepts of being and time. That is what we would be calling here a hauntology" (202). Derrida speaks of hauntology as a "conjuration," but, as Frederic Jameson notes, it does not mean we must believe in ghosts: "All it says, if it can be thought to speak, is that the living present is scarcely as self-sufficient as it claims to be; that we would do well not to count on its density and solidity, which might under exceptional circumstances betray us" (39). Hauntology makes us question our long-held assumptions of how things came to be and throws those assumptions into flux. Through the figure of the ghost that is neither living nor dead, present nor absent, it is a lens that helps us see reality more clearly. And because of its deconstructive powers, the hauntology of Philip's "Un" shakes the stable certainties of modernity and topples the mantle of being and presence upon which it is predicated.

To be sure, the prefix un marks a refusal, but it does not "fix" the language or the epistemic violence of the past, nor erase it, for that would be replicating colonial strategies of containment. As such, Philip's work refuses singular categories of being, but she is also keenly aware of the impossibility of total refusal—the spectre forbids it. In the Undex of these words, the words are still intact, though preceded by the *not* of the *un*. So, we may speak of the "unman," but the Man still haunts the language and the consciousness of how we came to be. Or, as Derrida puts it, "One never inherits without coming to terms with some specter" (24). Rather than overwriting or forgetting the past, the poetics of "Un" allows us to confront these specters—to confront their violence and silence in the present. These spaces between the narrative, as with the spaces of undoing created by the undone meaning of words in the text, make room for continued irrational untelling, for the haunting of things left untold or are still to come. Hence the queries of the Unpeople once the Time of Un is upon them: can they undark the light, unneed eachother, unblacken their skins? Hauntology thus marks this untimeliness of the present by manifesting unfinished events, multiple presents, and, as Reed puts it, the "forms of futurity and ancestrality for which we lack an adequate name" (29). For Philip, that adequate name is The Book of Un—her way of paying homage and acknowledging our obligation to these other, spectral, conceptions of being and time that allow us to imagine more just and possible pasts, presents, and futures.

The hauntology of *The Book of Un with Undex* moves beyond the reversal of language to reveal the deeply entrenched cultural amnesia brought about by the silencing Western gaze. As Philip tells Paul Watkins:

> We have been severed from indigenous cultures, names lost, spiritual practices outlawed; there is a sense in which you could say that shorn of all those things that make humans human, we become ghosts of ourselves, haunted by all that we know we know but can't remember, as well as by what we know we don't know and, simultaneously, spectral beings—duppies, zombies, or jumbies, inhabiting a world that is not truly ours—aware that somewhere out there in a parallel universe there is another world where we could become truly embodied, with embodied addresses, so to speak. ("We Can Never" np)

By opening language to the hinge of *Un*—by releasing verbs and nouns from their fixed definition, Philip's work revises and rewrites the past in her creation story about the Unpeople. She takes the colonial gaze, which determined slaves to be unhuman "unpeople," and unsaid this erasure with a vibrant narrative of agency, play, and love. Married with the transformative magic of experimental poetry, of making an unstable poetic object out of historical record and testimony, these haunting untellings become an unconcretizing and eroding force—one that eats away the deposits of material ontologies told to us, and unburies those spectral others that lie beneath the patina of singular truth and being. As a method, hers is nonlinear and nondeterministic; it is unpredictable and uncertain. Like the circular spin of the Rolodex, it is undone.

Untell: *Zong!*

Hauntology thus proves a useful term for poetic inquiry more generally, but specifically for diasporic explorations of time, being, and his/tory—the tidal waves of remembering and forgetting, being and nonbeing, longing and unrest. The haunted language of *The Book of Un with Undex* is a continuation of the poetics of Un threaded throughout *Zong!* that works to undo and untell—to take the deterministic language of colonial power under its spell and unsilence those held under it. In her Notanda to *Zong!* Philip characterizes her poems as "hauntological":

> I come—albeit slowly—to the understanding that Zong! is hauntological; it is a work of haunting, a wake of sorts, where the spectres of the undead make themselves present. And only in not-telling can the story be told; only in the space where it's

> not told—literally in the margins of the text, a sort of negative space, a space not so much of non-meaning as anti-meaning. (201)

Zong! "untells" the story of the slave ship *Zong* through its dissociative fugue and counternarrative, created by dismembering the untruths of the legal case surrounding the slave ship. As she writes, *Zong!* is "the Song of the untold story; it cannot be told yet must be told, but only through its untelling" (207). The hauntology of the text illuminates the fact that all that exists, exists alongside the haunting of excluded others—those absent presences that are yet to be born, those who are no longer and those who may never be.

The poems of *She Tries*, as with her work in *Zong!* are "unreadable in the traditional sense," ("Managing" 297) since they defy normative left-to-right reading practices. Philip's text is written using the language from *Gregson v Gilbert*, a 1783 insurance settlement case in which the owners of the slave ship threw a large number of slaves overboard to claim insurance money for the loss of "property." This decision of the court—the only public document in existence that testifies to the Zong massacre—cloaks the violence and injustice of the event in the logic of expense and proprietary loss. Equal parts eulogy and revisionary archive, Philip's text dismembers the logic-locked rhetoric of the law into a fragmented word store that mourns and gives voice to its overwritten voices. As the language and logic of the legal decision break down and fragment throughout the text, a fugue of submerged voices, sounds, silences, and stories surface in a visceral language of memory and affect. Throughout the text, the language breaks down in sense and typography, with the once blackened font becoming ever so faint and ghostly on the page:

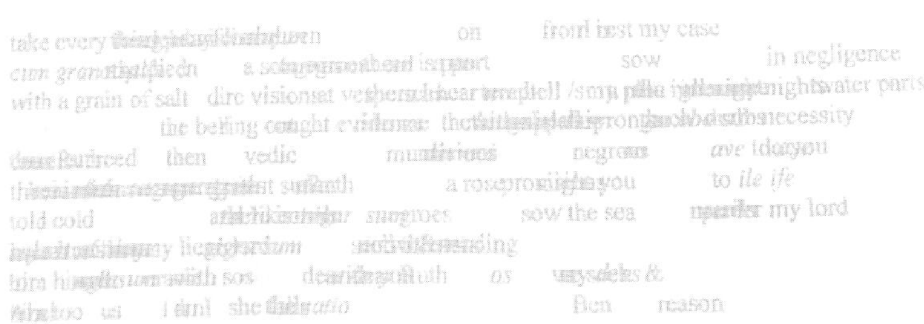

Figure 5. Philip, *Zong!* 182.

The words from this last section "Ebora" submerge meaning and sense in a watery fugue. In the Notanda to the text, Philip describes the rather haunted circumstances from which these palimpsestic, overwritten collages of words came about. She recalls her "laser printer for no apparent reason print[ing] the first two or three pages superimposed on each other—crumped, so to speak—so that the page becomes a dense landscape of text" (*Zong!* 206). The ghostly traces of words piled upon words create a dense fog of unmeaning and untelling; but in this fugue, the collective voice of those lost is brought to the surface, unsunk from the bottom of the sea.

His/tory's omnipotent, universalizing gaze lures us into forgetting that untold stories are present below the surface. In the same way that her poetics of Un haunts the human in *The Book of Un With Undex*, in *Zong!* Philip's language evades fixity, haunting rationality with its absent presence. Philip's fugues make these traces manifest in the watery expanse of the page; significantly, they resist apprehension and comprehension at times. This is because these stories rise to the surface after colonial waves have crested; their subaquatic swells undermine received histories and haunt the present with their unbeing. In this way, Philip's haunting poetic conjures what T J Demos, in his analysis of artistic responses to colonialism in Africa, calls "modernity's phantoms—that is, the disturbances and lingering presences, or presences of absence . . . through which current social formations manifest the symptomatic traces and uncanny signs of modernity's history of violence and exclusions" (13). For Philip, experimenting with prefixes, with form and space, with the imagination, allows us to see these spectres more clearly and to honour their presence. To heed the spectre is to understand that reality, language—indeed the world, as we know it—is undecidedly undone.

Unmanage: *She Tries Her Tongue, Her Silence Softly Breaks*

For Philip, language, form, and poetry more generally, have always been a means of being "unmanageable." She is a lawyer by trade, and so her entire poetic oeuvre is marked by a relentless interrogation of systems of order and categorization and a desire for unmanageability as a resistant poetic praxis. In her essay "Managing the Unmanageable," she writes: "In

She Tries . . . I set out to be unmanageable. I refused to 'know my place,' the place set apart for the managed peoples of the world. I intended to define my own place and space and in so doing I would come up against the role of language and the issues relating to that" (296). "Management" is a colonial practice used to keep bodies "in place"—or, as Philip defines it, "putting the unmanageable into preordained places within society so they can be more easily controlled" (295). Thus, she renders her texts "unreadable" to better register the experience of slaves as "managed peoples" (298).

In both *She Tries* and *Zong!* Philip's poetic techniques consist of dismembering and re-membering to undo and untell colonial order. As Brenda Carr notes about *She Tries*, many of the poems "signal linguistic intervention as the dominant gesture of her text" ("To 'Heal the Word Wounded'" 78). Working within language and form—both the words on the page and how they are arranged—Philip undoes the authorial surety of the Word and opens alternative pathways to understanding, articulation, and being. She works with language, which, as she argues, "traditionally had been yet another tool of oppression, a language that has at best omitted the reality and experience of the managed—the African in the New World—and at worst discoursed on her nonbeing" ("Managing" 296) Most of the poems in *She Tries* are concerned with the way language roots and nurtures us, like a mother, but also the way it entraps us and serves as a flimsy thing upon which to base our being. The first page of "Discourse on the Logic of Language," one of Philip's most anthologized poems, is indicative of this "unmanageable" poetic:

Discourse on the Logic of Language

WHEN IT WAS BORN, THE MOTHER HELD HER NEWBORN CHILD CLOSE: SHE BEGAN THEN TO
LICK IT ALL OVER. THE CHILD WHIMPERED A LITTLE, BUT AS THE MOTHER'S TONGUE
MOVED FASTER AND STRONGER OVER ITS BODY, IT GREW SILENT—THE MOTHER TURNING
IT THIS WAY AND THAT UNDER HER TONGUE UNTIL SHE HAD TONGUED IT CLEAN OF
THE CREAMY WHITE SUBSTANCE COVERING ITS BODY.

English
is my mother tongue.
A mother tongue is not
not a foreign lan lan lang
language
l/anguish
anguish
—a foreign anguish.

English is
my father tongue.
A father tongue is
a foreign language,
therefore English is
a foreign language
not a mother tongue.

What is my mother
tongue
my mammy tongue
my mummy tongue
my momsy tongue
my modder tongue
my ma tongue?

I have no mother
tongue
no mother to tongue
no tongue to mother
to mother
tongue
me

I must therefore be
tongue
dumb
dumb-tongued
dub-tongued
damn dumb
tongue

EDICT I

Every owner of slaves shall, wherever possible, ensure that his slaves belong to as many ethno-linguistic groups as possible. If they cannot speak to each other, they cannot then foment rebellion and revolution.

30

Figure 6. "Discourse on the Logic of Language," from *She Tries Her Tongue, Her Silence Softly Breaks* (1989) p.30.

Here, Philip plays with the white space of the page, with the Western English left-to-right reading pattern, and with dissonant discourses of logic to create a fragmented, multivalent collage. As Philip tells Coomi S Vevaina in an interview, "The Caribbean is a site of massive interruptions. . . . It seems to me that if I were to try and write that experience in a logical and linear way, then that would do to it a second violence" ("Searching for Space" 19). So, to undo the hold of this colonial violence, Philip transforms the space of the page into one of active play. The poem is arranged in three columns, with her poetic explorations of language placed in the space between the edict and the beginnings of a mythological matrilineal tale, one that reflects her origin story in T*he Book of Un with Undex*, where people are unburdened of historical silencing and given the tools of articulating their being.

It is worth noting that Philip's use of the prefix *un* is not her first foray into linguistic intervention using prefixes as metaphorical constructs for rehabilitating language and being. *She Tries* opens with Philip's essay "The Absence of Writing, or How I Became a Spy," which explores her concept of the "i-mage," another object of haunting linguistic play. Staging the i as a prefix, she notes, recalls the "Rastafarian practice of privileging the 'I' in many words," but it is also an act of radical healing:

> If what the artist does is create in her own i-mage and give *name* to that i-mage, then what the African artist from the Caribbean and the New World must do is create in, while giving name to, her own i-mage—and in so doing eventually heal the word wounded by the dislocation and imbalance of the word/i-mage equation. This can only be done by consciously restructuring, reshaping and, if necessary, destroying the language. When that equation is balanced and unity of word and i-mage is once again present, then and only then will we have made the language our own. (*She Tries* 21)

The "i-mage" of Caribbean people, the source of their self-expression and "heart of all life," has been dislocated by the colonial project, which broke their connection between the self and language, "the body bro- / ken" (44). "With the withering of the word in the New World," she writes, "not only did the i-mage die, but also the capacity to create in one's own i-mage" (14-15). Philip sees the role of the poet as critical in undoing this erasure, for in her work she must "translate the i-mage into meaningful language for her audience" (12). Her poetics of undoing, of fragmenting and re-membering, is a way of healing the i-mage of its break, of reconnecting the self to language and thereby bringing that self and those collective selves into being. This linguistic hinge of refusal and healing—of healing through refusal—has resonated throughout Philip's career. Within the flotsam and jetsam of *Zong!*'s untelling, within the legal language of loss and erasure, the collective voices and i-mages of the overthrown slaves are salvaged, unburied, and unsunk—and made to sing. Similarly, at the moment the girl nourished the seeds of the Story of Un in *The Book of Un with Undex*, the Unpeople were liberated to self-create in their i-mage—to unbegin, to unlive, to unbe.

Philip's work has often been associated with poststructuralist theories and the L=A=N=G=U=A=G=E school of poetry; however, she has been careful to articulate her intention and process differently. For Philip, experimenting with language will always be an act of survival, of embodied agency, and of subverting the colonial project. In her Notanda to *Zong!* she explains that her poetic strategies of dismemberment and fragmentation "signpost a multifaceted critique of the European project" (*Zong!* 197).[5] As Kevin Everod Quashie argues, "For [Philip], as for many Black writers, voice is metaphorical but also literal power, and what is at stake in the writing process is not only knowledge but also human livelihood" (131). The space opened by Philip's experimentations in language—even in the minutia of the prefix—hold a tension between knowledge, play, and survival. In the face of Western language that silenced, closed off, and fixed bodies in a gaze, she uses prefixes like doorways, pathways through, openings, and entrances.

By putting *The Book of Un with Undex* in dialogue with *Zong!* and *She Tries*, my hope here has been to showcase the continuation of Philip's poetics of Un from past to present. Philip's desire to undo Western Man's ontological and linguistic dominance is not so much a futile effort to undo the violence of the past or somehow get beyond history; rather, through her work from past to present, she occupies the space of the *un* as a space of refusal and resistance. But, following Wynter, this haunting poetic is also one of enchantment and creative undoing: the hauntology of Philip's poetics of Un offers a means for "capturing enchantment in a disenchanted world" (Gordon 8) while also doing the work of revealing injustices, undoing colonial practices, and seeking more just and human futures. Philip's poetics of Un resists seeing language as static and given, and instead imagines and creates in a space of possibility, of imagination, of agency. Her work from past to present teaches us that while undoing the colonial violence of Man is an impossible task, we can learn from it and employ other humanisms, other stories, other futures on the landscape and language of its sediment. In short, we can undo, untell, unknow, unbegin, anew.

SHANI MOOTOO

Male Monstrosity or Failed Masculinity? Shani Mootoo's Literary Oeuvre

Juan M Salomé Villarini

Shani Mootoo was born in Dublin, Ireland in 1957. Her parents Indra and Ramesh Mootoo returned to their native Trinidad when she was three months old. She grew up and lived in San Fernando, one of the larger cities on Trinidad's southwestern coast until she emigrated to Vancouver at the age of twenty-four. Mootoo is a novelist, poet, visual artist, and videographer, and her first book, *Out on Main Street*, a collection of short stories, was published by Press Gang in 1992. Four years later, Press Gang published her first novel, *Cereus Blooms at Night*. This was followed by her second novel, *He Drown She in the Sea* (2005), *Valmiki's Daughter* (2009), *Moving Forward Sidewise Like a Crab* (2014), and *Polar Vortex* (2020).

This essay explores the overriding theme of monstrous Indo-Caribbean masculinities in Shani Mootoo's works of fiction, which reaches its representational climax in *Cereus Blooms at Night* in the character of Chandin Ramchandin. In *Cereus Blooms at Night*, a series of incidents progressively pile up to produce Chandin Ramchandin's degeneration and dehumanization, which are foreshadowed by Chandin's embarrassment towards his parents' status as indentured labourers and his desire to distance himself from their Indianness. Instead, under the white tutelage of Reverend Thoroughly, Chandin's identity becomes increasingly dependent and embedded in the patriarchal need of recognition from others, particularly the devotion and admiration of women in his life, which he does not receive (6).

The domination of women as the cornerstone of the identity of Indo-Caribbean men and the manifestation of monstrous masculinities is a traceable theme even in Shani Mootoo's early fiction. In her short story *A Garden of Her Own*, one of nine stories in the collection *Out on Main Street*, Mootoo creates a sense of impending danger within the walls of the apartment where Vijai lives with "the husband" (15-16). In this cramped "bachelor apartment" Vijai lives with a steadily escalating sense of foreboding that her actions may have the "potential for blame," and that anything she does might raise the wrath of "the husband" (15-16).

Vijai's use of the definite article "the" rather than the possessive adjective "my," to refer to the man she is married to, gives the phrase "the husband" a cold, detached connotation stripped from any kind of affection, but retains the implication of the authority and ownership "the husband" has over her (15-16). This looming feeling of harm yet to come is strongly evident when at "five-thirty, Saturday morning" Vijai debates if she should get out of bed and face "the husband," or if she should remain in bed, which either way could have negative consequences for her (15). If the following quote was read without context, the reader might be inclined to imagine that it is a scene from a horror story or film in which a monster, a serial killer, or a rapist is about to pounce on its victim.

> Then there was a space empty of his sounds. The silence made the walls of her stomach contract like a closed-up accordion. Her body remained rigid. Her heart sounded as if it had moved right up into her ears, thundering methodically, and that was all that she could hear. She struggled with herself to be calm so that she could know where he was and what he was doing. (17)

Vijai's sense of fearful entrapment within her marriage and the cramping walls of the "bachelor apartment" she inhabits with "the husband" is accentuated by her growing expectation of harm coming her way (11). Even when "the husband" directs Vijai "to the edge of his bed" their sexual contact is devoid of tenderness (11, 17). Instead of an act which brings consummation to their marriage, their sexual intercourse is an act of ownership, a forceful taking of her person as "her body is crushed under his as he slams himself against her, from behind, grunting" like an animal or a monster, and "she holds her breath, taut against his weight and the pain, but she will not disturb his moment" (23).

The theme of a tyrannical and violent Indo-Caribbean masculinity is also evident in "Lemon Scent," the second story in *Out on Main Street.* Kamini is viewed by her husband, "as his prized exquisite accomplishment, [the] envy of his men friends," which he "must not lose" (26). For her husband, Kamini is a possession, a commodity, a trophy that heightens his reputation; his social life revolves around "those men he works with and parties with" and not Kamini, whom he keeps secluded at home (30). On the nights when Kamini's husband is out with "those men," Anita spends evenings with Kamini and eventually they become lovers (30).

Suspecting Kamini and Anita are having an affair, her husband whispers to Kamini: "If I ever find out that you two have slept together I will kill you both" (Mootoo, *Out on Main* 28). Kamini's husband is concerned about his reputation and his standing before his "men friends," which would be tarnished if he loses "his prized exquisite accomplishment" (26). The theme of the Indian wife in middle- and upper-class Indo-Caribbean society as a commodity and trophy, an enhancement to prestige yet often dismissed and unimportant to their husbands is an element of the domineering and menacing masculinity that permeates Mootoo's work.

In Mootoo's novel, *He Drown She in the Sea*, attorney general Shem Bihar, a. k. a. "Boss," as everyone, including his wife. Rose Bihar is often "written about . . . in the women's section of the paper as the prime example for all women in the Caribbean," hailed as the woman "other women should strive to be like . . . a mother whose children c[o]me first and who [stands] behind her husband, no matter what" (252), a role that she has played for many years. Yet eventually she, who has mostly served the role of a societal staple for her husband, decides to leave him and go to Canada to become reacquainted with a childhood friend with whom she has fallen in love. However, when her husband becomes aware of her intentions, "He take out a thick-thick bundle of dollar bills from his pocket and throw it at her, shouting that he himself would pay her passage. But when she say all right, she want to leave, he get vex, he start to cry, to beg, he shout, he threaten to take his own life, and Madam say okay, okay, she not going anywhere" (295).

Shem Bihar's manipulation tactics, which ricochet from anger to tears, to supplication, and back to threats, are driven by his fear of losing standing and power within the upper-class society he belongs to. "You have no shame? He is a gardener. You gone crazy? You need to check your head. You want to bring shame on us?" (295). Rose is disgusted by her husband's hypocrisy. "Shame?" she retorts. "Who brought shame on this family? Not you? You are the one who is out almost every night with some woman hanging from your elbow" (295). Men like Shem Bihar, who exhibit vulnerable and fragile Indo-Caribbean masculinities in Mootoo's fiction, depend on how chaste their women are seen to be by their communities, in order to keep their untarnished male respectability. Without female chastity, respectability is unattainable for these men.

Notoriously unfaithful to his wife, Shem Bihar is willing to kill her and her friend Harry to avoid the dishonor and humiliation of being left by his wife. In Shem Bihar, Mootoo embodies a susceptible, cowardly, and spoiled false masculinity that pretends superiority but cannot subsist without his wife's performing her role of submission and devotion towards him.

> Look here, you playing with your life if you think you going to make a fool out of me. You want to bring shame on us? You forget who have the police and the law on his side. You wouldn't live a day to shame me, you hear? And that yard boy—no place is far enough for him to hide from the kind of people who loyal to me. Hear me good: I will not let you or him destroy my family name. (297)

Shem deploys a calculating, murderous masculinity; he stops at nothing to protect his threatened honor. Rose's only chance to escape is to fake her death, and so she stages her drowning in the ocean. Only death could liberate her from her husband's ownership and allow her to have a "fresh start" with her childhood friend Harry St George (15). "Oh God, get help, Piyari, get help quickly. Oh God! A riptide. Madam got caught in a riptide. She just went under. She hasn't come back up" (300). Eventually, Harry and Rose end up together, but not without a great deal of pain and danger.

In Mootoo's work there is a consistent presence of men for whom the domination and control of the sexuality of women are directly proportional to the reputation and respectability of their manhood. However, the presence of Indian women in continuous battle for autonomy and control of their sexuality is also evident. The dilemmas of Mootoo's female characters are reminiscent of those of the indentured Indian women of previous generations; just like them, Mootoo's women dangerously resist and fight "to maintain their relative degree of autonomy" (Reddock, "Freedom Denied" 79).

It is worth mentioning at this point that Mootoo also creates alternative masculinities in her fiction which are not violent and dependent on women's submission for their self-esteem. As Frantz and Rennhak point out, "When women construct and write about men in fictional worlds, not only do they analyze the causes and effects of patriarchy, as Woolf does in *A Room of One's Own*, but they also construct their own realities, imagining alternative masculinities that are desirable from a woman's perspective" (2). In all of her novels, Mootoo accomplishes the task of representing "desirable" masculinities "from a woman's perspective" (2) that are in contrast with the men perpetrating violence against women in her novels.

The Monster in *Cereus Blooms at Night*

It is in Mootoo's first novel, *Cereus Blooms at Night*, that we find the condensation and the most grotesque and violent representations of the monstrous masculinity that infuses her depiction of many Indo-Caribbean male characters in her fiction. Although Chandin Ramchandin's behavior cannot be called anything but atrocious, we encounter in *Cereus Blooms at Night* a detailed historical background that helps the reader predict the sources and circumstances that trigger Chandin's behavior. To begin with, Chandin grew up in the plantation barracks, where his parents were laborers, and where sexual and physical violence were prevalent against Indian women, although this issue is not directly addressed in the narrative. Chandin "had been born just before [his parents] left India," therefore the gender relations between his parents could presumably have mirrored the traditional patriarchal expectations in India of women's subordination to men (26). There is one instance in the narrative to support this view.

When Reverend Thoroughly arrives at the Chandin quarters in his "horse and buggy" to visit them, Chandin's mother "quickly [pulls] her orhanie over her head and nose and mouth, and [hurries] around to the front" (27). Women's veiling is associated with their seclusion from other men and shows female modesty and decorum, and it is done to uphold family honor, particularly that of men, by "desexualizing the female body and removing women from public view as objects of temptation for men" (Mohammed, "Gender Relations" 393-394). Growing up in a household where his mother was expected to uphold family honor through the decorum of her dressing could have also influenced Chandin's view that women must always dress modestly when in front of men and act subserviently. Additionally, another aspect of Chandin's upbringing that is suspect is the way Chandin is viewed and treated by his father. When "old man Ramchandin" hears "the crunch of gravel and the ruckus of a horse and buggy maneuvering the dusty path" he wakes up from his daydreaming and faces "[t]he harsh reality of his two-room ajoupa quarters in the barracks. His two thin cows were yet to be tied up for the approaching night. He was exhausted. He could have told Chandin to tie up the cows but he considered the task too menial for the gold bead of his life" (27).

"Old man Ramchandin" wants something better for his son. He does not want his son to live the same life of servitude he has. He believes, therefore, that educating "Chandin out of the fields" approximates his son to a Brahminical status and may liberate him from "his inherited karmic destiny as a servant laborer" that he had thought he could leave behind through "the long journey across two oceans" (26, 27). The fact that Chandin's childhood and early adolescence were spent in the barracks where social and gender relations, and sexuality itself were often expressed through violence can be seen as potential precursors of Chandin's violent sexual behavior as an adult, which become further complicated by his adoption by Reverend Thoroughly, his relocation from the barracks, and the deracination he undergoes through Presbyterianism.

Chandin Ramchandin is, undeniably, "a moral monster" in all senses of the term (Foucault 81). He rapes both his pre-pubescent daughters, Pohpoh and Asha, after his wife Sarah abandons him to elope with her lover Lavinia. The rapes take place in their house and are known to the Indian community, which does not come to the girls' rescue. Neither do Reverend Thoroughly and his Presbyterian followers, some of whom are members of Chandin's Indian community. Mootoo points at the hypocrisy and narrow thinking of the community as follows:

> Living had become a matter of habit for Chandin Ramchandin. He began his day as usual walking from house to house calling out, "Madam! Madam! Boss! You need help today?" He had learned to avoid some houses. Their inhabitants would come out wielding a broom, shouting to him to get away, that they did not want the likes of him around their children. While many shunned him there were those who took pity, for he was once the much respected teacher of the Gospel, and such a man would take to the bottle and to his own child, they reasoned, only if he suffered some madness. And they further reasoned, what man would not suffer a rage akin to insanity if his own wife, with a devilish mind of her own, left her husband and children. Whether they disliked him or tolerated his existence, to everyone Chandin was Sir. (195)

The community blames Sarah and Lavinia's eloping for what has happened to Pohpoh (Mala) and Asha and justifies Chandin's behavior as a natural result of his humiliation. Mootoo echoes here the prevalent theme in the fiction of Indo-Caribbean women writers such as Ramabai Espinet and Lakshmi Persaud, among others, about the silence that often accompanies sexual violence against women in the Caribbean.

In Persaud's *Raise the Lantern High*, Vasti Nadir witnesses the rape of one of her schoolmates. "When I left childhood behind, the memory of the rape I had witnessed became an invisible companion, bringing constant distress to my adult life. There was no one with whom I could share this experience . . ." (3). In Espinet's *The Swinging Bridge*, Mona Singh witnesses how her uncle Baddall sexually assaults her mother. "I hated Muddie for letting Uncle Baddall touch her. Would she tell Da-Da? She should tell Da-Da, and he should curse Uncle Baddall upside down . . . But I knew that Muddie would say nothing; nobody in our family ever said anything about anything" (38). In *Cereus Blooms at Night*, Chandin Ramchandin's character can be read as a case study in the psychological trauma that results in the evolution of monstrous Indo-Caribbean masculinity. The first trigger of Chandin's degeneration is his loathing of the fact that he is the child of indentured laborers, which leads naturally to self-loathing.

An early indication of Chandin's progressive self-loathing is that he feels ashamed by his mother's presence when the Reverend arrives at his father's quarters to finalize his adoption. Chandin is mortified by "his mother, smelling of coals and charred eggplant and a sweat that embarrasse[s] him with its pungency of heated mustard seed" (27). The rejection of his mother marks the beginning of Chandin's scorn towards all that is Indian, especially women, and consequently his eventual desire for a white woman, Reverend Thoroughly's daughter, Lavinia.

After Chandin "left the barracks he was not inclined to return" and "he hardly saw his father but his mother went to church services at least once a week, especially to see him sitting up there in the front" (29). This must have been very difficult for her, since Chandin sat in those occasions "right next to the Reverend's wife," now Chandin's adoptive mother (29). Seeing his mother at church makes Chandin hope his mother might embrace Christianity. However, "the few times he [goes] to the barracks to visit," he realizes that this will not be so. "When he [inquires] after the foot long brass crucifix the Reverend had given her to put above the doorway, she shyly [says] that she had wrapped it carefully in a clean white cloth and put it away" (30).

In contrast, Chandin notices that "the number of statues of Hindu gods and goddesses lining the walls [has] increased since his move to the Reverend's house," which makes him realize that his mother has "not really converted to Christianity" and she never will (30, 31). These episodes seal his alienation from his mother and further his distancing from the emotional life of his Indian heritage. The last few times he visits his parents at the barracks, the "faint cloud of pooja smoke" that permeates "his parents' hair and clothes" while performing their "Hindu prayers" revives Chandin's repulsion towards their Indianness, and triggers the memory of "the odor of coals and spices that used to emanate from his mother's body" before his adoption, and his embarrassment returns and increases.

Chandin stops visiting them altogether (30). By completely severing his ties with his parents, he tries to establish a new identity that is not hyphenated to Hinduism or his parents' Indian identity. His goal is to fully break away from his roots, which he hopes to accomplish by living with the white Canadian missionary family of Reverend Thoroughly. Living with the Thouroughlys, Chandin comes face to face with the apparent economic and social advantages of learning English and turning Christian, when he becomes surrounded by "upholstered" chairs and mesmerizing "chandeliers" with shimmering "leaf-shaped glass pendants," and "fine cabinets, carved chairs and side tables and lamps with fancy shades" (31). "In his innocence" Chandin seems to conflate "the Reverend's faith" with the Reverend's "taste" and economic status and seems to think he will be able to achieve one through the other (31). He sees "his people's lack of these [material] things" as the "result of apathy and a poverty of ambition." He is unaware that the position of "his people" is predetermined by a colonial hierarchy in which Indian laborers occupy the last place and must remain there to secure the economic and racial status quo in Lantanacamara's colonial society (31).

Thus, surrounded by the material lavishness of the Thoroughly's house, Chandi's alienation from his origins is sealed, for he now feels an "immense distaste for his background and the people in it" which inevitably ends ups being directed at himself for he cannot escape his Indianness and the stereotypes that are read upon his "darkly-brown Indian" body (32, 34). Just as Frantz Fanon is momentarily crushed by the objectification of the white French gaze, by its othering and the negative response to his Blackness, Chandin Ramchandin is crushed by the objectification of his Indianness (82), which constructs him as an outsider to the white society he wants to belong to, and as a backward heathen who needs to be saved. Besides, Chandin lives in a society where his skin color and physiognomy makes him unsuitable to seek the affection of a white woman.

In front of the mirror, Chandin's "darkly-brown Indian" body tells him he is Indian, that he looks like "the other boys in his class and from the barracks in the fields" which he hatefully acknowledges but never accepts (34). Fanon embraces his Blackness: "Some identified me with ancestors of mine who had been enslaved or lynched: I decided to accept this" (*Black Skin* 85), but Chandin falls prey to self-hatred and an impossible desire to efface the colonial indenture discourse which is written upon his "darkly brown" body and his "blue-black hair" (34). He increasingly begins "to hate his looks, the color of his skin, the texture of his hair" and "his accent," all which he views as permanent obstacles to becoming recognized as one of the Thoroughlys.

This racial self-loathing becomes another of the triggers that further dehumanize Chandin's identity and unleash his sexual pathology. Desperate to escape his body, he anxiously concentrates his efforts on changing "what he ha[s] the power to change" and begins to closely observe and imitate Reverend Thoroughly's behavior and manners (34).

> Chandin took note of the Reverend's rigid, austere posture, so unlike his own father's propensity to bend or twist or fold his body whichever way the dictates of comfort tipped him. He practiced sitting upright, with his back unswayed and his legs planted firmly on the ground or crossed severely at the knees. Other times he diligently studied and imitated the Reverend's pensive stroking of his chin or tapping of his fingers against a book. (34)

Chandin not only tries to copy Reverend Thoroughly's demeanor and behavior, but he also tries to command the same authority the Reverend projects. Thoroughly is a patriarch who dominates his wife, his daughter, his congregation and students at the seminary, and that is the aura Chandin also wants to cast.

However, the realization that he will always be an outsider to the white Presbyterian community he has been transplanted into becomes bitterly clear to him. Although he "seemed to be well liked by the taller, fair, heavily accented men . . . he wondered constantly whether it was because he was the Reverend's adopted son . . . or because he was of the race that it was their mission to Christianize" (38). His isolation, now that he has no contact with his parents at the barracks, continues to increase when he moves "into quarters at the seminary some miles away" from the Thoroughlys' home (38). "Chandin was the only person of Indian descent at the seminary. He was in fact the only non-white person there. He and seventeen other men lived together in the institution's dormitories. The others had all come from the Shivering Northern Wetlands" (38).

His mental state worsens when Reverend Thoroughly rejects him as Lavinia's suitor because he is her stepbrother. "Look here. You are to be a brother to Lavinia and nothing more. A brother. She is your sister and you her brother . . . you must not have desire for your sister Lavinia" (37). This verdict shatters Chandin's world.

Years later and now a man, Chandin believes he has accomplished a degree of prestige, respectability, and "whiteness . . . related to class" and "social standing" through his education and graduation from the seminary (Tate and Law 89). He is also convinced that he must once and for all make his feelings for Lavinia be known to her before "someone with more aplomb . . . step[s] in and steal[s] her away" (39). So Chandin declares his love to her: "Lavinia, listen to me please. I think only of you. I have only ever thought of you. I must tell you that I love no one quite as much as I have always loved you" (41). Lavinia's response is clear and devastating: "No! No! No! This is ridiculous . . . Don't speak a word of this to anyone, Chandin. Please. I disapprove and do not consent—" (41). Shortly after their conversation, Lavinia and her parents leave for the "Shivering Northern Wetlands" to visit their relatives and Chandin spends the holidays alone and miserable (38, 42). His feelings of rejection are further compounded by the realization that the Reverend has rejected him as Lavinia's suitor because of he is Indian and not because he is her so-called stepbrother.

When he finds out that Lavinia will marry her white cousin "Fenton Thoroughly," he renounces his dream of marrying her. However, he has learned through his upbringing in the barracks and his observations of the Thoroughly household that marriage is part of being a man, and a wife is a necessary acquisition to have a respectable public image (44). Thus, since Chandin cannot have the woman of his dreams, he settles for marrying the next best choice he can think of. " 'I, I, it's time for me also, I have been thinking of Sarah. Sarah, you know Sarah.' Chandin wanted nothing more than to collapse in the security of a woman, a woman from his background, and Sarah was the most likely possibility" (45). Mootoo's representation of Chandin as needing "to collapse in the security of a woman" hints at Chandin's dependency on a woman's admiration and approval for his self-worth (45).

As mentioned above, a dependence on the procurement and domination of a chaste woman to assert their masculinity to themselves and the men in their community is the cornerstone of the psychological make-up of the monstrous masculinity of Mootoo's male characters. Chandin marries Sarah, and they conceive two daughters Asha and Pohpoh. Eventually, when Lavinia returns to Lantanacamara after her prolonged stay at the Wetlands, her friendship with Sarah, who had been her schoolmate, is rekindled. Lavinia's frequent visits to the Ramchandin's house gives Chandin some hopeful joy, especially when Lavinia develops close ties with his daughters Asha and Pohpoh. Chandin once again attempts to close the gap between him and Lavinia, but she only spends "some token minutes with him" and when Chandin complains "to Sarah that Lavinia [is] losing interest in him even as her brother," Lavinia begins to avoid Chandin's presence altogether (56).

As time goes by, Sarah and Lavinia fall in love and "they no longer [try] to conceal their closeness from Pohpoh and Asha" (56). Chandin becomes increasingly suspicious of this intimacy. One day at the beach while taking a picture of his family and Lavinia, Chandin notices how "Lavinia place[s] herself behind [Sarah], and he [sees Sarah] press herself against Lavinia. Through the lens [Chandin] watche[s] carefully and [sees] Lavinia's hands rest tenderly on [Sarah's] waist" (58). Chandin confronts his wife Sarah about her affection for Lavinia, and the two women "have no choice but to make a decision" and plan to elope and take the children with them overseas (59). "There were already two trunks atop the buggy, strapped down with thick leather belts" when Chandin unexpectedly returns to the house and notices "the pictures missing from the walls . . . that the curtains [are] drawn, that the house [is] uncommonly tidy" and Chandin realizes what is going on (63). He might have undergone education and learned the teachings of Christianity, but he cannot erase his upbringing and growing up in the barracks out of which his "patriarchal male psyche" had been forged, and which disables him from coping with the situation (Natarajan xvi). Thus, Chandin is not only an incestuous rapist but he is also a "*monstrum*," "that which warns", "that which reveals," the mental disorder that both his inherited Indian "patriarchal male psyche" and the white Presbyterian masculinity he adopts produce in him (Cohen 4; Natarajan xvi).

Lavinia, Sarah, and the two girls would already have been gone when Chandin arrived, but Pohpoh (Mala) had forgotten "her bag with all the seeds and the shells and the cereus cutting" and had gone back inside the house (63). She could not get out of the house in time and Chandin got hold of her. In the confusion that arose with "everyone shouting at once," Asha, who was still at the buggy, calls for her: "No! No! No! Pohpoh! Pohpoh, Pohpoh. I want Pohpoh." Lavinia and Sarah release her and both girls are left behind with their father (63). Full of rage, Chandin "rifle[s] through the photographs, pitching some on the floor", and "those of his wife or Lavinia Thoroughly he crumple[s] into a ball, then [spits] on, all the while crying and making growling sounds," and then throws "the crumpled photographs into the kitchen sink" and sets them on fire (64). Chandin has lost complete control of the objects of desire that had barely held his manhood together until this point. Burning their pictures symbolizes and foreshadows the revenge he will carry out against them through sexual violence towards his daughters.

At this stage in the dehumanization of Chandin's identity, his daughters become just bodies, sexual objects that he can possess in the name of revenge. In T*he Unsafe Sex* Natarajan describes "three kinds of public violence" towards twenty-first century Indian women, in which "rape" is used "as a weapon"; one kind involves violating the "body of women to assert . . . power" or, in Chandin's case, to give vent to his powerlessness in an Indian community which sanctions the degradation of Indian women and looks the other way (xii).

> One night he turned, his back to Asha, and in a fitful, nightmarish sleep, mistook Pohpoh for Sarah. He put his arms around her and slowly began to touch her. Pohpoh opened her eyes. Frightened and confused by this strange, insistent probing, she barely breathed, pretending to be fast asleep. She tried to shrink away from under his hand. Suddenly, awakening fully, he sat up. Then he brought his body heavily on top of hers and slammed his hand over her mouth. (65-66)

Chandin has now degenerated into an incestuous rapist, a monster (66).

The horror and monstrosity of Chandin's behavior intensify for the reader when it becomes clear that raping his daughters is not an isolated incident, but an atrocity that becomes his routine. Unlike Rose, in *He Drown She in the Sea*, who must fake death to free herself from her husband, freedom and autonomy are not an option for Pohpoh as long as she is near her father. Therefore, in an act of self-preservation Mala (Pohpoh) crushes her father's head by repeatedly slamming a door on it (229). Although free from her father's sexual and psychological abuse, Pohpoh's trauma is irreversible, and she remains mentally ill for decades, only to experience some improvement at the end of the narrative.

Many of the Indo-Caribbean female protagonists in Shani Mootoo's literary oeuvre are surrounded by a sense of danger and impending doom, which emanates from the frail, domination-driven masculinities of her Indo-Caribbean male characters. The failure to accomplish female domination ensues a violent feeling of shame and dishonor in them. The challenges of Mootoo's female characters are not very different from those faced by their forebears during indenture in the Caribbean. Like their forebears, they seek individual, economic, and sexual freedom, while preyed upon by men.

Mootoo's *Cereus Blooms at Night* gives us a historical and psychological framework to understand the origins and nature of this monstrous Indian masculinity, which viewed indentured and postindentured Indian women's quest for autonomy and self-sufficiency as unchaste behavior, and for which they were mutilated and killed. Furthermore, Mootoo's literary oeuvre also reminds us that this form of Indian masculinity is not a thing of the past but remains alive in the present century.

JENNA BUTLER

Postcolonial Ecologies and Sustainable Living: Reading Jenna Butler's Nonfiction

Asma Sayed

> When we love the Earth, we are able to love ourselves more fully. (bell hooks, "Touching the Earth")

Ecocriticism, also known as literary ecologies or environmental humanities, is the study of literature and the environment, and has been a fast-growing field gaining momentum in the 1990s. Postcolonial ecologies intersect the histories of colonialism and environmental imperialism as a way of moving beyond the accusation levelled at postcolonial studies as being an anthropocentric field ignoring the issues of ecological reconfiguration brought about by colonialism and industrial consumerist capitalism. Thus, postcolonial ecologies is the alliance between postcolonial studies and ecocriticism. In their perceptive and well-articulated introduction to the collection of essays, *Postcolonial Ecologies: Literatures of the Environment*, Elizabeth DeLoughrey and George B Handley envision postcolonial ecologies as the broadening of the complex "genealogy for thinking through our ecocritical futures and a turn to a more nuanced discourse about the representation of alterity, a theorization of difference that postcolonialists, ecofeminists, and environmental activists have long considered in terms of our normative representations of nature, human, and otherwise" (9). In 1978, William Rueckert, created the term "ecocriticism" to frame "the grounds upon which the two communities—the human, the natural—can coexist, cooperate, and flourish in the biosphere" (107). To him, ecocriticism, earlier referred to as environmentalism, blossomed in the 1970s and 1980s within a predominantly Anglo-American romantic representation of the natural environment, going back to the Romantic poets and the transcendentalists. He defined it as the "application of ecology and ecology concepts to the study of literature" (107). Cheryll Glotfelty and Harold Fromm explained it simply as "the study of the relationship between literature and the physical environment" (xviii). Richard Kerridge argues that an "ecocritic wants to track environmental ideas and representations wherever they appear, to see more clearly a debate which seems to be taking place, often part-concealed, in a great many cultural spaces. Most of all, ecocriticism seeks to evaluate [practices] texts and ideas in terms of their coherence and usefulness as responses to the environmental crisis" (5). Accordingly, Greg Garrard sees ecocriticism as "the study of the relationship of the human and the nonhuman throughout human cultural history and entailing critical analysis of the term 'human' itself." Garrard further reasons that "Ecocriticism is unique amongst contemporary literary and cultural theories because of its close relationship with the science of ecology" (5). The incorporation of ecocriticism into the humanities and literary studies is further defined by Glotfelty and Fromm as "an earth-centred approach to literary studies" (xix), through which ecocritics explore the "cross-fertilization between literary studies and environmental discourse in related disciplines such as history, philosophy, psychology, art history, and ethics" (xix). Garrard also insists that as a field of study that draws inspiration from the humanities, social sciences, natural sciences, and moral philosophy, ecocriticism naturally transgresses other disciplines.

This essay engages ecocritical theories to examine the work of Jenna Butler, a Canadian woman of color and writer, who, through her narratives, fosters an understanding of the impact of human actions on the environment from postcolonial ecocritical, ecopsychology, and deep ecology perspectives. Butler's work reflects her alignment of literary postcolonial ecologies with environmentally conscious living.

Early ecocritics or literary environmentalists, began to reread the nature poetry by English Romantic poets such as William Wordsworth, Percy Bysshe Shelley, John Clare, and Samuel Taylor Coleridge. Lawrence

Buell's studies of American literary transcendentalist writers such as Ralph Waldo Emerson and Henry David Thoreau in his foundational works, *The Environmental Imagination: Thoreau, Nature Writing, and the Formation of American Culture* (1995) and *The Future of Environmental Criticism: Environmental Crisis and Literary Imagination* (2005), set the stage for literary scholars to seek answers beyond the Romantics' and Transcendentalists' apprehensions about the rise of industrialization and urbanization and the loss of the wilderness as a place of solitude and human recuperation, to an exploration of the representations of European expansion and colonization of other environments by theorizing this as postcolonial ecocriticism. As Glotfelty and Fromm state, in its early days ecocriticism was predominantly a white male movement and they hoped that as it grew it would expand to become more of a "multiethnic movement [with] stronger connections . . . made between the environment and issues of social justice" (xxv). Other known proponents include Graham Huggan and Helen Tiffin who in *Postcolonial Ecocriticism: Literature, Animals, Environment* (2006) deal with issues of ecojustice as they expand on the human-animal relationship. In contemporary times, many writers, including Amitav Ghosh and Robin Wall Kimmerer, have raised concerns about climate change and the loss of traditional ways of living, not just as a result of the damage to the natural ecologies by unsustainable and unregulated industrialization, but also as a consequence of cultural colonization by Europeans. These writers and ecocritics focus on examining the human relationship with non-humans and the impact of human pursuits on ecosystems. In Canada as well, many writers, both Indigenous and settler, have written about landscape and surviving in the wild (Soper and Bradley 2013). Jenna Butler writes from the historical experiences of formerly colonized landscapes of Tanzania, India, and Canada. Her work and life stand out in tangent to other writers because of her exemplary commitment to sustainable and ecologically conscious living that reflects in her writing. She is not just intellectually and romantically concerned with ecological crisis, but does something personally about it in her little space through organic and sustainable farming practices.

Butler is a poet, essayist, editor, and professor. She is the author of three books of poetry, *Seldom Seen Road*, *Wells*, and *Aphelion*; two collections of ecological essays, *A Profession of Hope: Farming on the Edge of the Grizzly Trail and Revery: A Year of Bees*; and the Arctic travelogue *Magnetic North: Sea Voyage to Svalbard*. Much of Butler's work focuses on the environment, climate change, and sustainability. A woman of British and South Asian-East African heritage, Butler brings forth a distinct feminist lens to her discussion about the climate crisis, and takes her inspiration from other nature writers such as Wendell Berry, Lois Hole, Barbara Kingsolver, Patrick Lima, Eliot Coleman, as well as Thoreau and Kimmerer.

Butler's life and literary works, which centre mostly on the landscape and the environment, take into consideration the deep ecological approach whereby she questions the neoliberal aesthetics which value economic progress at the cost of human life, health, and dignity and lead to climate change and destruction. Deep ecology

> affirms an understanding of life in which the thinking of the 'self' must already include other organisms, and all that supports them, as part of one's own identity. Recognition of this 'greater self' must entail an ever-widening circle of identification with other living things. A viable 'self' is not the atomistic individual of liberal capitalism, for which the whole world is a source of possible self-gratification and assertion. A biocentric ethic emerges in the perception that to kill another creature is in some sense an act of violence against oneself. (Clark 24).

Butler lives off-grid and grows produce and raises bees while being mindful of her ecological footprint on the surrounding environment. Living through Canadian winters in the boreal forest, Butler thinks about the land she lives on and the way its historical context ties in with her writing: "I also wonder if the Canadian aesthetic consideration of place and space is the result of being a blended country with a number of influences at work: Aboriginal narratives of land, culture, and belonging; settler narratives of displacement, change, and rooting; and recent influxes of immigrants and refugees, whose narratives often take the form of stories about lands and homes lost, left behind, and the necessity of new groundings" ("Contributor Spotlight").

This chapter will focus specifically on Butler's three nonfiction accounts about climate change: *A Profession of Hope, Revery*, and *Magnetic North*. In these books, Butler explores capitalist systems of living from an ecological point of view and argues that if we are to save the environment for our next generations, we need to act now and move toward a sustainable way of living. She critiques the anthropocentric view and the human colonization and control of the natural world and the neoliberal, capitalist projects which have done irreparable harm to the planet. By sharing her personal journeys of travel, farming, and bee-keeping, Butler centres discussions about climate change, grief, and hope and reminds her readers that the only way forward is to live with the land and nature in harmony and mutual respect. Thus, Butler's literary texts are a warning and an ecocritical intervention pushing to embrace deep ecological thinking and ethics of care.

A Profession of Hope

A Profession of Hope chronicles Butler's farming journey. In 2006, Butler and her husband, Thomas, who until then had mostly lived a city life, bought a piece of uncleared land in Barrhead, Alberta to start small-scale organic farming. In this book, Butler takes the readers with her on her extremely arduous journey of converting part of one hundred and sixty acres of untamed land into a productive space, Larch Grove Farm, in that part of the world where temperatures dip below forty degrees Celsius. Starting an organic farm in the middle of a cold zone involves working long hours, patience, and hope. Butler herself has been allergic to the mass-produced chemical-ridden food available in super markets. Thus, she decided to grow her own food as much as possible. She narrates the process of clearing the land, digging ponds, chopping wood, buying seeds and solar panels, cooking off a wood stove, canning and freezing produce, and the day-to-day challenges of living off the grid. This experiment in regenerative agriculture soon became a lifelong commitment. As she built her home on the farm, and worked with a community of like-minded people, she also thought about the way the contemporary capitalist modes of producing our food are non-sustainable, harmful, and unethical. Butler is deeply concerned about the genetically modified food that we consume and the way our agricultural practices are not only non-sustainable but also dangerous for us: "our poisoned food is deeply symbolic of our skewed way of interacting with the land around us" (21). Sustainable farming also requires patience and extremely hard work. She is aware that "It's a frightening thing to leave behind the chemical-filled world of 'perfect' food that we grow up with in the West and go the organic route, where you are very much aligned with nature. We are, on this continent in particular, great fans of the quick and easy" (21).

Butler critiques the anthropocentric view that humans can and should control nature; she sees this kind of relationship as colonial and argues for a biocentric perspective:

> Our every interaction with an increasingly threatened environment needs to become one where we meet at an interface. Over destruction can no longer be the norm, because we very truly are in this together—every living thing. We can't take back the damage we've inflicted, but with effort, I do believe we can change it, as long as we are willing to give up our notion of being at the top of the power pyramid. Let's face it: things are dire, and there is no hierarchy in this struggle for survival. (120)

She makes every attempt to ensure that her farming does not alter her environment in a negative way, working *with* the land rather than on the land. It is equally important to think about saving the land and the environment for the generations to come, and one way of doing that is to take an organic approach. This approach, Butler argues, "looks at leaving this land in a better state than we found it for the people who will come after us to think in terms of generations" (30). As she builds a sustainable infrastructure around the farm, she immediately starts seeing changes. Many different kinds of wild birds return to the space: "As the ecosystem in the garden area shifted from dead willow thicket to verge landscape with forest edge, the variety of birds broadened" (98). She receives the birds, those that stay all year round and seasonal visitors, as a way to understand the changing seasons and build a relationship with the nonhuman world.

Butler presents a biocentric view in the book. According to Timothy Clark, biocentrism "affirm[s] the intrinsic value of all natural life and displace[s] the current preference of even the most trivial human demands over the needs of other species or integrity of place" (2). Butler asserts, "The human and natural worlds are points on the same continuum, not blips on two tracks running parallel to one another, destined only occasionally to conflict with static-like bursts of friction leaping the lines" (115). Basically, she believes in working with the land and living with it rather than simply profiting from it. This requires taking only what is necessary, being careful not to hurt it, and replenishing it without using pesticides or other chemicals.

In order to foster sustainable living, Butler argues, we need to look at Indigenous ways of living and traditional ecological knowledge. To build a relationship with nature, one needs to listen to it. In a conversation, she said:

> We need a deep sense of listening. Listening to Indigenous cultures and approaches to land guardianship that have been in place for much longer than many colonial relationships with land. So, listening to wisdom that has been there for a very long time, expanding our willingness to listen to one another and dialogue and learn from one another, and also [develop] a sense of listening to the land itself: what is sustainable? . . . A major listening shift needs to happen. (Sayed)

Nature also provides a place and a space to heal. In the chapter titled "The Memory Gardens," Butler recounts her family history as it moves from Tanzania to Britain to Canada. A patch of her land is reserved as a memorial to family members who have moved on. With its selection of flowers and scents this garden allows her to embrace grief and to heal. She plants lavender for her British grandmother, roses for her grandfather, and irises for a friend. Migrating across continents and generations means leaving friends and family behind, not being able to visit them or their graves. Sitting by the memory garden Butler remembers and counts the dead; this is the space where she and her husband "can go to remember . . . [and] grief loses its claws when there's a patch of ground in its name" (34). The pain of diasporic displacement and separation eases in the lap of nature. The gardens "offer [them] food and calm, [and] they also offer [them] solace" because their dead are "in many, many grounds" across the globe (35). Planting flowers and vegetables is a way to remember, she says, "there's an aesthetic of loss in that. But we also plant for life and continuity" (36).

Revery: A Year of Bees

Continuing with the preoccupations of *A Profession of Hope*, in *Revery: A Year of Bees*, Butler contends with beekeeping, climate grief, and trauma recovery. The term "climate grief," Butler writes, "became a recognized term increasingly used to describe the loss of hope and the feelings of helplessness experienced by many in connection with human-created climate change" (107). An anthropocentric view of the world puts human beings at the centre, and everything else is valued only in relation to its usefulness to them. This way of thinking has only harmed us. As Butler moves around on her farm, she sees humans as part of a complex, interconnected world. The sights, sounds, and smells of her farm include the music of bees humming and swarming while searching for nectar. Butler explains to the reader the world of bees, the way they live in harmony with nature, and how she sees them as our educators and our hope for the future.

Butler provides crucial information about an industry that is not much known. In the chapter titled "Sweet White Gold," she gives us the long history of the honey industry in Alberta, the world's fifth largest producer of honey, a fact not as widely known as the province's oil and gas industry. Another interesting detail is that the bee industry is increasingly being led by women. The bees feed on canola, clover, rapeseed, and other crops. They pollinate all the fields they are placed in, thus also helping the farmers, but large-scale corporate agriculture and the use of pesticides are disastrous for the bees and also the environment. Butler argues that unless industries are "called to account for their impact on this world," we will not be able to confront climate change (87).

The bees are living organisms with their own ecosystem and a relationship with humans that is not always comprehended until one builds a rapport with them. They communicate with humans in ways that can be understood only if they make an active attempt to. Butler writes about how she could not get closer to the hives if she was stressed or worried as the bees sensed negative energy and were not welcoming. In that sense, bees are her teachers. They have "taught [her] about ecosystem balance, the desire to grow naturally and without chemicals, and the value of good food to our community" (85). More importantly, the bees have taught her about healing, as they have a "calming impact" on her and have forced her to face difficult situations: "Beekeeping has taught me that if I want to become effective at what I do, I need to become more determined to confront the darkness I carry within me. Every breath of negative energy I can shed makes me kinder, more benign, and this is reflected in the health of my hives" (85-86). Beekeeping, tending to the hives, and being mindful of the surrounding, helps Butler see the natural world and the way it connects to the human world. It helps her "to recognize that, at the end of the day, we are all interconnected, interdependent. None of us lives in isolation, and every one of us stands to gain from recognizing our role as part of a larger, sustaining ecosystem" (96). She reminds us that "[T]he keeping of bees is a blending of science and spirit; a passion that is, at its roots, an act of hope" (16).

The book is, in many ways, about "solastalgia," or climate grief. Occasionally, the author senses despair: "periods of deep disillusionment that little we do here, on this farm we've been building for the past sixteen years will have any real impact when faced with worldwide climate crisis" (116). Yet there is a desire for transformation. Butler cites Senator Murray Sinclair and reminds her readers that rather than feeling guilt and grief, we should focus on shame, which is more powerful in pushing us to make a change. As much as she grieves for what we have lost and are losing to climate change, she also yearns for a better and sustainable future.

Magnetic North

In *Magnetic North*, Butler takes her readers on a journey to the Svalbard archipelago off the coast of Norway. She visited the islands on an ice-class masted sailing vessel as a writer-in-residence with other artists from around the world. Over a period of two weeks, Butler observed the impacts of environmental changes and global warming on the endangered islands. The book, a blend of poetry and lyrical prose, brings together her concerns about her home environment in the boreal forest and the effects of climate change in the Arctic. At home in Alberta, she worries about fossil fuels and forest fires; in the Arctic as she hears glaciers falling apart and sees melting permafrost and rising sea levels, she worries about the future: "To watch a glacier calve is to watch time run in both directions at once . . . Calving is a funny thing, birth and death gnarled inseparably" (72). She is alarmed at how the archipelago is changing: "The new berg is a small knell for the glacier cracking its spine along the strait. Each summer a little thinner, ice bruised by a malignant swell of mountain coming clear beneath. In a scant decade, there will only be rock; the swaybacked ridge of the glacier will be as much a memory as the whale pods darkening the inlets along Svalbard's flank" (72). The signs of damage were visible as soon as she arrived there: "Everywhere we looked, we saw human intervention etched onto the land in the form of mine ruins, processing effluent, and piles of whalebone" (xi). And later, she writes, "What we are capable of when we hollow the earth, small gods with hammer and tongs, refineries and their atmospheric smear. In our hands, Vulcan's desire to fashion in his own image, a cacophony of voices forming under his fingers. A face pinched from the clay, distant muttering from a tight-jointed box. Bright-eyed Pandora and her cargo of assassins" (74).

In the section titled "Threads," Butler further shows the interconnections between the boreal and the archipelago. In Svalbard, "PCBS on Billesfjorden, Pyramiden leaking its slow veins out to sea . . . Oil pollution from the storage ships wrecked at Kappa Laila"; in Alberta, "380,000 litres of condensate [poured] into grizzly habitat at Grand Cache. 4.5 million litres of crude into the muskeg by Little Buffalo. Half a million litres of sour crude into the Red Deer River. 230,000 litres of crude onsite at Elk Point. 60,000 litres of crude and hydrogen sulphide gas into the muskeg at Red Earth Creek" (78-9). In spite of oil spills on such large scales, "*Regulators say, wildlife not affected*" (79). This irony upsets Butler. Although there have been "Two crude oil spills a day in [her] home province [Alberta], every day since 1975," the capitalist oil industry and the government work together and are not affected by the long-term impact of oil spills as long as it "doesn't directly impact homes, economies" (80). The comparison of the boreal to Svalbard that Butler presents in the book is essentially a reminder that our lives are connected across continents and what happens in one part of the globe has direct or indirect consequences for the other. A globalized world has its advantages, but when it is a matter of the environment, dependence on the global may not be the best course of action. As she mentions in the two books discussed above, one needs to create local infrastructures and think locally while being aware of the global impact of environmental destruction.

In all three books, Butler writes with conviction, honesty, and concern, and she argues that one needs to accept the grief so that one can then move on to the next stage of hope and change. She encourages us to relearn and reclaim our skills of ecological perception as theorized by ecopsychologist Laura Sewall (201-15). That way, the hurt of the earth will be heard and responded to for our healing. The settler-colonial, capitalist, and extractivist agendas have done much harm to our ways of living and we need to think biocentrically and move towards living sustainably. While the books serve as warnings about the rapidly changing climates, and portray a deep concern about the future of our planet, they also present hope that we will turn things around and work towards healing and making this world a better place. In that sense, Butler is one of the modern-day Romantics. She urges us to use decolonial methodologies, to seek guidance from Indigenous knowledge and elders, and to find ways to work with the land in order to stop environmental destruction. Respect for the land, nature, and all living creatures needs to be at the centre of our relationship with everything on this planet.

CLAIRE HARRIS

Witnesses from the Silentiaries: Claire Harris's Poetics of En(Dis)abling in *dipped in shadow*

Dannabang Kuwabong

> . . . / write
> for us all we must change
> the fictions before the fictions
> play us out their unsubtle denouements
> skies without cloud
> earth without rivers or smiles.
> (*dipped in shadow* 93)

At the end of *dipped in shadow*, these lines encapsulate Claire Harris's creative philosophy. To wit, poets are narrative witnesses to the silent traumas in sociocultural relationships. Claire Harris (1937-2018) immigrated to Canada in 1966 from Trinidad and set up residence in Calgary, where she died in 2018. Her books of poetry include *Fables from Women's Quarters* (1984), *Translation into Fiction* (1984), *Travelling to Find a Remedy* (1986), *The Conception of Winter* (1989), *Drawing Down a Daughter* (1992), *dipped in shadow* (1996), and *she* (2000). Gingell describes Harris's poetry as preoccupied with "racism and sexism in Canadian society [. . .] imaginatively and excruciatingly represented" (143). She points out that Harris's neglect in Canadian literary scholarship stems from her postmodernist experimental style posing a substantial intellectual challenge to readers (143). Also, Susan Rudy asserts that Harris's poetry is "not just [about] her life but also for her life" (94). Additionally, Rudy claims that Harris "speaks out against the potentially unravelling oppressions of race, gender, and class in contemporary Canada, refashioning poetry, narrative, autobiography, and the English language itself in the process" (94-95). Sylvia Adams in a similar vein, presents Harris's poetry as lamentations "at the festering sores of human crisis and tragedy, in particular at their effect on women in a society that is paternalistic and frequently brutal" (1996, qtd. in *Voices from the Gaps* 2009). In this essay, my reading of *dipped in shadow* echoes these concerns and styles of representation.

George Elliotte Clarke has counselled against reading Africaribbean Canadian women's poetry solely through the lenses of race, gender, sex, and ethnicity. I embrace his call for a reading praxis that accepts that Harris's poetry is "upsettingly, even cruelly, apolitical and illiberal enough to analyze how blackness and womanhood remake syntax, grammar and diction to yield undeniable excellence" 163). Indeed, *dipped in shadow* showcases Harris's continuous rejection of prescriptivist and didactic poetry, often seen in poetic "sermons against racism, sexism, imperialism, classism, and homophobia" (164). In her reading of Harris's poetry and other Black Canadian women poets, Lynette Hunter problematically concludes that for Harris, "race and racism are among the most important issues for the Black writing community in Canada, and any of its readers" (256). Unaware of her diminishing of Harris's contribution to Canadian letters, Hunter then explores Harris's poetry as material for sociological research to understand what it means to be Black and female in Canada. Even when she includes Harris in her discussion of Canadian postmodern poets, she dismisses her through a convoluted logic based on Harris's race and presumed foreignness (256-259).

Harris's so-called use of experimental poetry traces back to the influences of Caribbean oral poetry in dialogue with European poetic traditions: "Poetry began as an oral form—in all aspects—from regular rhythm to rhyme . . . Paper, the page, has become part of it. I wouldn't dream of publishing with someone who proposes altering my poems . . . I have combined several forms to say what has to be said. And I deliberately make it possible to read down and across . . ." (117). Instead of being defined through the postmodern traditions engaged by other Canadian poets, Harris's poetic style is a dialogue between European literary traditions and the traditional African Caribbean ways of seeing and presenting ideas. This dialogue disorients readers looking solely for evidence of racism in Harris's poetry.

In response to the racialized reading methodology, Harris argues that her poems "see-through see / beyond scenes of culture/gender/race / to persons . . ." (93) and signify "in en(dis) abling difference" (93). To "en(dis)abling difference," Harris advocates an embrace of what Edward Kamau Brathwaite calls "total expression" (273), a practice found in oral poetry: "The oral tradition . . . makes demands not only on the poet but also on the audience to complete the community, the noise and sounds that the poet makes are responded to by the audience and are returned to him" or her (273). As Adams argues, Harris's complex word arrangements act as scaffolding for the complex intersections of various human evils, ranging from "domestic abuse to maternal relationships, to incest, war, and mental health" outside and within the contexts of race, gender, class, ethnicity, and nation (Adams 1996). In *dipped in shadow*, as in her other books, Harris's word and stanza arrangements on the page ". . . make the reader feel as if" they are reading and hearing "different languages, voices, and personalities all within one person" (Gingell 144). The reader is given a chance through white spaces in which he or she can rearrange the poem's puzzle pieces to produce meaning. Reading Harris involves reading her poems aloud and observing how the eyes rearrange the stanzas into predictable poetic forms that convey Harris's politics.

Emily Williams identifies Harris's political engagement as intersectional rebellions against the evils of "(pedophilia), violence, war, and disease (specifically AIDS)" (188). For Harris, the "atrocities that women are . . . subjected to and to which they subject themselves" (188) are best exposed and critiqued through poetry. Harris's themes are all-inclusive. She shows no preferential focus on "gender, race, culture, or political entity blameless, [but] challenges her [readers] with passion and often brutal detail to move beyond the pain caused by these situations toward a reparation of the ills and away from the silent and participatory stance" (188).

The poems in *dipped in shadow* are stand-alone. Yet they come together as traumatic experiences endured by subordinated people in communities: women, young people, children. Harris begins with a roll call of women's groups differentiated by colour, race, ethnicity, class, and origin. This roll call is a direct interrogation of the differences that keep women apart. The woman is a "Strong sister [is] cloistered in her story / Clothed in her skin" (9). She asks Black women, "when I / insist on my seeing, do you call me *traitor* / cut eyes at me[?]" (9). In turn, she challenges white women for their racism. On "Yonge and Spadina when [they] see our / black brother" (9), "do you draw your skirt closer / cross at the corner / my sister my friend?" (9) And she asks Asian women whether they "fade to dream Asia away / from [their] sistersm wear caste as armour" (10).

Continuing with Asian women, the poet asks a Chinese sister, when "at late bus stops a man shouts *black / cunt*" (10) does she dissociate herself from her black sister, "grumbling in the gleam away from / your sister kind sister dear friend?" (10). She calls on Cinnamon-skinned women to speak up when they read about "white brothers in pedophilia our daughters" (9). White women writers must answer why they shut out immigrant writers from the canon. "And you forest sister plains sister / what haunts you in your sun wheat skin / when I cry out for space for air" (10). These accusations refute feminist claims of universal sisterhood.

Following these accusations against the sisterhood rhetoric, the poems in "O WHAT ARE YOU THINKING MY SISTERS" (7-12) parade several witnesses to testify that the divisions among women help normalize pedophilia and physical and sexual violence against women and children of both sexes. Consequently, Harris frames her arguments on the absence of a united front by women to effectively fight the systemic violence women and children face. The greatest obstacle to this struggle is patriarchy, the legal system, and negative social and familial responses to those who would dare publicly expose these abuses against women and children. Constrained by these fears, women sometimes demonstrate violent rage, accomplishing "what years of prayers, petitions, and protests cannot: it gets you taken seriously" (Philip 319). In "NUDE IN AN ARMCHAIR," Harris dramatizes a mother's problems as she attempts to liberate herself and her children from an abusive, pedophilic ex-husband and his friends. The legal system, loaded against women's rights, rules against her, thus helping to perpetuate the violence and abuse.

In her testimony in court, the woman lists a litany of gruesome abuses. On the first Saturday of every month, the father—once a devoted family man—brings home his upper-class friends, including the local mayor, and takes them with his kids to the basement. The scene radiates with "the lascivious / gleam of . . . husbands / while in a corner a nude / boy played the flute" (26). His younger sister supposedly dances a ballet, a euphemism for lap-dancing. We observe how men exercise predatory sexual powers over children. The words "lascivious" and "gleam" add significance to the pregnancy of the girl. The wife's fears are doubly confirmed. Dark spaces in the basement provide cover for the sexual violation of the children, contrasted. sharply with the empty whitespaces on the poem's page, and uppercase letters tower over lowercase letters in the same word: "yOurs." Emily Williams argues that the uppercase O's use elicits several interpretations: it represents the hollowness of the father, the mother's pain, and the children's defenselessness.

To cope with her distress, the mother stages tea parties, attended by her ex-husband and his friends, including the mayor. She compares herself with Jael, the Hebrew woman who saves Israel by murdering Sisera, the commander of King Jabin's enemy (*The Holy Bible*, Judges 4:17–24; 5:24–31). She sees herself lacking the courage of Jael and lapses into feeble verbal protests: "i say the kids want to stop / you turn their lessons your eyes / flare the air is begging my body hovers" (20). The man responds with his belt. This assault reopens wounds from her childhood when her father abused her. Telling the man, "over your buckle the belt circles / . . . / burns your brown shoes scarred like my father's" (20), she becomes again the cringing, crying, sobbing, baby (20).

Her daughter eventually becomes pregnant and seeks an abortion. In the process of giving consent, the mother becomes the one accused of the daughter's condition. Finally, she acts—does something that is a secret—and faces criminal charges in court. Though the crime remains a mystery, everything points to homicide. In court, she is blamed, mocked, and scolded by the judge. He accuses her of enjoying her ex-husband's abuses. "I put it to you that you enjoyed those beatings. That you were a willing participant . . ." (21). Why did she not try to escape?—to which she retorts, "where could i go that he couldn't / find me? how would we live? i / phoned the police they said no lock . . . would they / be better off if i were dead" (22)? None of this touches the judge.

	Q:	
the room	You are under oath. surely at that	*courtswells*
muffles	point you knew that something was	*shimmer*
your	terribly wrong?	*discordant*
secrets burn		*a nutcracker*
naked	A:	*seizes*
i didn't know	it was not the first time i had been	*how could i*
floors hover	beaten	*know*
the air		*the judge's*
is dead	Q:	*webbed wings*
zone my	You expect us to believe that your	*cling*
father's faces	husband would beat you simply for	*to my hair*
are bear	saying that your children no longer	*frozen*
traps faces	wished to take ballet/to play the	*i*
swing crazily	flute?	*lungs stuffed*

The arrangement of the poem in columns visually depicts the court scene, highlighting at the same time the effects of an insensitive legal system on victims of domestic abuse. The left and right columns in italics reflect how testimonies of abused women are rendered inconsequential. The verse arrangement with white spaces has a purpose: "I never protest against a page—all that lovely white space. If you can always reread it. It's hearing that is limited. Moreover, what's there is not simply three poems. It depends on whether you read across for one line or two, then down, then up again, then across again, then down." This "gives you choices, and you would be surprised by what you'll find once you do that. Moreover, it hedges the form on the page, and it constricts and strangles the speaker in the centre, especially where it is used as ritual" (119).

Harris explains that the "play of language and space"—whitespace, capitalization, punctuation, repetition, right justification, and scattering of words and lines in what appears to be a haphazard arrangement—grants her the flexibility to "say a great deal and suggest a great deal more" about what social issues trouble her. She distorts syntax as a challenge to see how far concealed and coded meanings can be squeezed out of the grammar imposed "by a [colonial] culture that conspired to erase [hers]" (Williamson 3). To "say the unsayable one needs to distort, to break down, to open up the words to find out what they contain" (Williams 3) and provide alternative views.

Whitespaces are moments of retreat from the dominant white noise of the spoken word—paginated white spaces issue moments of contemplation of alternative histories and positions. Nigel Thomas, in an interview with Harris, asks her whether the "silences" signified by the white spaces are "implicit statements" (118); whether they "contextualize sound, are important, so that they may be shaped by silence on the way" (118). Harris explains that these spaces are "meant to shape, to interrogate meaning as well as history. . . . what has happened to one human being can happen to another again and again" (119). White spaces are the imaginary entrances into the closed worlds of abused women and children. They illuminate the suffering of the woman and her children in the poem. Through syntactic distortions, Harris gives voice to the abused and marginalized, inserting them into the public domain.

While Harris in "NUDE IN AN ARMCHAIR" is a critique of patriarchy, "SISTER (y) OUR MANCHILD AT THE CLOSE OF THE TWENTIETH CENTURY" critiques women's collusion with patriarchy in raising violent men to defend greedy capitalism. Mothers promote the warrior figure as the ideal of masculinity: "Dream warrior day after day my sister watches / him haunt weathered grass his face defines time / into sight stalk still kill his small body" (53). The boy gradually is emptied of all empathy through indoctrination into warrior consciousness. He is "stripped with shadowy leaf with stem crouched / . . . / down into maleness her *beautiful man who kills*" (53). The mother's deliberate blindness to see the transformation of her son into a savage is unnerving. She "watches him day after day carving away chunks of / soul of tenderness empathy awe each day more / hollow . . ." (53). She suddenly becomes aware that by joining the army, her son has lost his reason and soul. This awareness is evidenced by the son's lack of human compassion and morality as he joins in the invasions of Grenada, Panama, Somalia, Afghanistan, and Iraq. These wars cause massive environmental and human destruction. The poet, as a witness, interprets these invasions as the continuation of the colonial wars of conquests (55).

Harris argues that contemporary Western militarism is in line with Kipling's white-saviour complex as developed in his book *The White Man's Burden: The United States and the Philippine Islands* (1899) to justify colonization as a civilizing mission. Nothing has changed: "my sisters the white man's / burden is still borne / on the backs of" (57) all people colonized by Europeans. The West's "civilizing" wars are conducted not to "make the world safe" or bring democracy to the oppressed. Still, it simply is a pretext to facilitate the "exploitation by Europe North America whoever / else the floundering raft may hold" (57). There is stress on how mothers raise their sons in ignorance to see war and aggression as games. Consequently, these sons become oblivious to the damage done to both foreign and domestic populations in war: "Sister I say it though saying it is terror / we suffer the ignorance of those who never bombed those / never poor we suffer those who lack imagination" (59). The descendants of invaded and enslaved peoples join in the wars against their ancestral homelands.

In "THIS FIERCE BODY," Harris reflects on the effects of the HIV/AIDS pandemic on marginalized gay and poor communities. The poem depicts the rapid decline of a healthy young gay boy, infected with HIV by an older man, probably a priest he trusts. Ignorant and all-trusting, the boy yields his body without protection: "despite / this fierce body / i arrive without weapons" when the man calls, "sudden without pity" (*dipped in shadow* 35). The boy knows that "something has happened to the air / [when] you say *i am*... gesture vaguely / pluck at the bedsheets... *AIDS*" (35). But concerned more about his respectability, he commands the boy to keep the secret (35). Sentenced to silence, marginalized, and made invisible by his infection, the boy enters into a life of lonely homelessness. The poet, bearing witness, asks, "who would not weep" at the sight and story of this once healthy young man (37)? To assuage his guilt feelings, instigated by his Catholicism that preaches against homosexuality, the priest redoubles his devotional practices: masses, confessions, penances, novenas, etc., but these rituals no longer give him peace. His health deteriorates rapidly; his joy, his happiness, and his future are all gone.

In "THIS FIERCE BODY," Harris lists the uncaring and immoral ways governments, churches, and pharmaceutical companies behaved towards the HIV/AIDS pandemic during the late twentieth century:

> that week full of third page headlines small rumours of plague
> war
> godwrath: Genesis of Plague Deaths Lack of Money Vaccines
> No use Condoms Biblical Condemnations Test Proposals
> Drugs
> Users Source of Infection Isolation Suggestions Gloves
> for Police Forces Lack of Research Firings School Pickets Gays
> March Promiscuity Heterosexual Population Threatened
> Blood
> Transfusions Infected Gay Man Charged With Spreading Virus
> in Tears Babies Born Wonder Drug in Mexico Wonder Drug in
> Paris Wonder Drug in The Bahamas at home Advertisements
> To Be Reviewed Too Explicit Truth Not in Interest of
> Population
> Law of Internment As Public Danger Passed MLAS' Raises
> Pass Lack of Interest Lack of Money no lack of hellfire/fear.
> (47)

Here she refers to the negligence of the Red Cross in giving Hepatitis C- and HIV-infected blood transfusions to Canadians in the 1980s. And she takes a swipe at the Catholic Church's uncompromising and unsympathetic stance on condom use in the face of HIV/AIDS.

Returning to the theme of pedophilia in "WOEMAN WOMB PRISONED" (63-93), Harris questions the romanticization of motherhood. Disillusioned by the negative experiences of teen motherhood, Jenny introspects about what it means for a girl "fifteen & committing / birth alone nine months ridden down to / silence" is not "trapped in rock" of social and cultural constructs from which escape is near impossible" (66). She recollects, "The first time He [her father] came to her tickling / she grateful for play in the pink and white / Room tickled back" (72). Without a mother figure to guide and protect her, Jenny is confused and unsure of how to handle her father's attention. Her story echoes the fifteen-year-old boy's story in "THIS FIERCE BODY" and the daughter in "NUDE IN AN ARMCHAIR." Her father calls her her a prostitute and a sinner. Raped daily, she gets pregnant several times, aborting or smothering the babies shortly after giving birth, fully aware of the risk. Should her father discover the truth, she intimates, "he would smash at her / another fault in his earth . . ." and denounce her for a "too fertile body" (73). Jenny is acutely aware her mother fled the house from fear of her husband's reaction to her aborted, adulterous pregnancy.

Jenny compares her predicament to that of Lot's daughters in the Bible. After Lot's wife turns to a pillar of salt for disobeying Yahweh's command, the daughters get their father drunk and rape him to make sons for him: "the younger arose went unto her father he perceived / not when she lay down nor when she arose" (76). But unlike Lot's daughters, whose actions carry no guilt or condemnation, Jenny is an unwilling victim of her father's rapes and God's judgement. Like the woman and her children in "NUDE IN AN ARMCHAIR" and the teen boy in "THIS FIERCE BODY," she is unable to flee or speak out. If she does, "He will find a way . . . to kill her He will beat . . . her / body shudders erupts words" (76). Jenny can only cry in the silence of her pain.

The poem spotlights child abuse, pedophilia, religious and moral hypocrisy, and rearguard tactics against oppression in atmospheres of extreme suffering. It ends with a restatement of Harris's feminist philosophy. It is not ceaseless marches and placard-waving that will free women and children from abuse. They are only liminal spaces for letting out steam, designed and allowed by control systems for the oppressed to feel that they have agency.

dipped in shadow undercuts the argument that Harris is mainly concerned with race and black femininity in Canada's racialized spaces. Her theoretical *poiesis* of fragmentation plays with her photographic use of light and shade to accentuate the paradoxes of social, cultural, religious, and political realities. The contradictions make the facts seem unreal. Each poem in *dipped in shadow* recuperates women's and children's voices from loud silences. Silence, represented by open white spaces, the deliberate distortions of normative stanzaic and word arrangements in poetry, reflect contradictory moments of both a disablement of the victims and strategic resistance.

In response to Nigel Thomas's question about what she thinks is her role as a writer (115), she said, "The primary job, I think is a groping towards truth, towards the real. Whatever I can find in spinning that is the world. I think the reality is obviously viewed as a construct" (115). She saw her work as crafting a "new vision to suggest another way of seeing to people who haven't had to do this; who in fact have no way of thinking about this . . ." (115). Governed and defined through a male "grammar of the sexes," she says, women develop a fluid grammar of dissent. Grammatic fluidity facilitates intersectionality, a dance of silence, word sound, and image across the page and society without political howling (91). Her poems reveal the terrifying consequences of inequality, war, and poverty on marginalized communities. Injustice, she contends, originate from the "social and economic, the historical and environmental fractures . . . constructed over" the past five hundred years (27). The oppressed, especially the women, "have had to fight back . . . Besides, I wanted to find out what happens when people violate their ethical principles" (27). Whether in domestic spaces or public arenas, dipped in shadow expose and critiques any violence, whether against women and children or vulnerable and emerging nations, as immoral.

Notes

Haunting the Human: M NourbeSe Philip's Poetics of Un

1. "M NourbeSe Philip / The Book of Un with Undex" np.

2. "Some Notes on Silence" 415.

3. I'm thinking here alongside bell hooks, who argues that "Postmodern culture with its decentered subject can be the space where ties are severed or it can provide the occasion for new and varied forms of bonding" (31).

4. In this way, Philip's haunting reversal of the events of history is reminiscent of Martin Amis' novel *Time's Arrow* (1991) in which he narrates the events of the Holocaust in reverse such that doctors in death camps heal patients, guards give prisoners jewelry, and bodies are revived by gas pellets.

5. In "Managing the Unmanageable," Philip expresses a similar sentiment of rupturing language as a power structure in *She Tries* while recalling Wynter's decentering of Western Man: "Working through the poems . . . resulted in an epistemological break for me; my relationship with Western European traditions . . . and systems of knowledge has been irrevocably ruptured. The understanding of how the underpinning of knowledge is often nothing but power—power of the white European male to define his knowledge as absolute—was a painful but liberating experience" (299).

References

Pamela Mordecai's Literary Transcultural Eschatology

Back Cover. *de book of Mary*: A Performance Poem by Pamela Mordecai, Mawenzi House Publishers Ltd., 2015.

Batcos Bennett, Consuella. "Jamaican Creole: Nuff Respec." *Changing Currents: Transnational Caribbean Literary and Cultural Criticism*. Edited by Emily Allen Williams and Melvin Rahming, Africa World Press, 2006.

Birbalsingh, Frank. "Review." Mordecai's '*subversive sonnets*' rocks the boat. Keeping Alive the Ties that Bind." cmc.journals.yorku.ca.pdf.

Clarke, George Elliott. "On Pamela Mordecai's "Passion Plays": A Plea for Their Performance." *Studies in Canadian Literature / Études en littérature Canadienne*, vol. 44, no. 1, 2019.

Duncan Wielzen. "Evangelization For a New Caribbean: A Renewed But Ongoing Reflection," *Justice and Peace in a Renewed Caribbean: Contemporary Catholic Reflections*, edited by Anna Kasarfi Perkins, Donald Chambers, et al., Palgrave, 2012.

Forbes, Cordelia. *From Nation to Diaspora: Samuel Selvon, George Lamming, and the Cultural Performance of Gender*, U of West Indies P, 2005.

Glissant, Edouard. *Poetics of Relation*. Translated by Betsy Wing, U of Michigan P, 1997.

Griesinger, Emily. "Toward an Eschatology of Literature." *Christianity and Literature*, vol. 53, no. 2, 2004, pp. 203-231.

Griffith, P. *Afro-Caribbean Poetry and Ritual*, Palgrave, 2010.

Hall, Stuart. "Introduction: Who Needs 'Identity'?" *Questions of Cultural Identity*, edited by Stuart Hall and Paul du Gay, Sage Publications, Reprint,1996, pp. 1-18.

Mordecai, Pamela. *de Man: a performance poem*. Sister Vision, 1995.

—. *de book of Mary A Performance Poem*. Mawenzi House, 2015.

—. *Certifiable*. Goose Lane, 2001.

—. *Red Jacket*. TAP Books, 2015.

—. *Pink Icing and Other Stories*. Insomniac Press, 2007.

—. *Subversive Sonnets*. TSAR/Mawenzi House, 2012.

—. "Pamela Mordecai: On Heart Language and Performance Poetry. Interview with Annick MacAskill" *Room: Literature, Art, and Feminism*, vol. 42, no. 1, 2019. https://roommagazine.com/interview/pamela-mordecai-heart-language-and-performance-poetry. Accessed March 27, 2020.

—. "Interview" with Nigel H Thomas. *Why We Write Conversations with African Canadian Poets and Novelists*, edited with an Introduction by Nigel H Thomas, Mawenzi House Publishers, 2006.

Perkins, Anna Kasafi. "Introduction: The Caribbean, Shaped by the Call for Justice and Peace." *Justice and Peace in a Renewed Caribbean: Contemporary Catholic Reflections*, edited by Anna Kasarfi Perkins, Donald Chambers et al. Palgrave, 2012.

Reiss, Timothy. *Against Autonomy: Global Dialectics of Cultural Exchange*. Stanford UP, 2002.

Richards, J. "In What Language do you think?: a case for the development of bilingual corporate worship in Jamaica." *Groundings*, vol. 27, 2012, pp. 30-38.

Savory, Elaine. "En/Gendering Spaces: The Poetry of Marlene Nourbese Philip and Pamela Mordecai." *Framing the Word: Gender and Genre in Caribbean Women's Writing*, edited by Joan Anim-Addo, Whiting and Birch, 1996.

—.Savory, Elaine. "Pamela Mordecai: Jamaican Language, Local and "in Foreign," *Beyond the Canebrakes Caribbean Women Writers in Canada*, edited by Emily Allen Williams, Africa World Press, 2008.

The Holy Bible. King James Version, The World Publishing Company, nd.

Volf, Miroslav. *Exclusion and Embrace: A Theological Exploration of Identity, Otherness, and Reconciliation*. Abingdon, 1996.

Watkins, W. B. C. *An Anatomy of Milton's Verse*. Archon Books, 1965.

Wielzen, Duncan. *Popular Religiosity and Roman Liturgy: Toward a Contemporary Theology of Liturgical Inculturation in the Caribbean*. Koln: Lambert Academic Publishing, 2009.

W H Hudson's English Argentina And Pablo Urbanyi's Argentine Canada

Borges, Jorge Luis. "El escritor argentino y la tradición." *Obras completas*. Emecé, 1974.

—. "Sobre The Purple Land." *Obras completas*. Buenos Aires: Emecé, 1974. 733-36.

Díaz, Roberto Ignacio. *Unhomely Rooms: Foreign Tongues and Spanish American Literature*. Bucknell UP, 2002.

Frederick, John T. *William Henry Hudson*. Twayne, 1972.

Gómez, Leila. *Iluminados y tránsfugas: Relatos de viajeros y ficciones nacionales en Argentina, Paraguay y Perú*. Iberoamericana, 2009.

Graham-Yooll, Andrew. *The Forgotten Colony: A History of the English-Speaking Communities in Argentina*. Hutchinson, 1981.

Huberman, Ariana. *Gauchos and Foreigners: Glossing Culture and Identity in the Argentine Countryside*. Lexington, 2011.
Hudson, W H *Far Away and Long Ago*. 1918. Intro. John Galsworthy. Dent, 1967.
—. *Green Mansions*. Intro. John Galsworthy. New York: Knopf, 1944.
—. *Idle Days in Patagonia*. AMS, 1968.
—. *Tales of the Pampas*. Creative Arts, 1979.
—. *The Purple Land*. 1885. Intro. William McFee. The Modern Library, 1927.
Jurado, Alicia. *Vida y obra de W H Hudson*. Fondo Nacional de las Artes, 1971.
Lorenzin, María Elena. *El humor como resolución de lo imposible en la obra de Pablo Urbanyi*. Pliegos, 2007.
Martínez Estrada, Ezequiel. *El mundo maravilloso de Guillermo Enrique Hudson*. 1951. Beatriz Viterbo, 2001.
Ronner, Amy D. *W H Hudson: The Man, the Novelist, the Naturalist*. AMS, 1986.
Urbanyi, Pablo. *El zoológico de Dios*. Catálogos, 2006.
—. *El zoológico de Dios II*. Catálogos, 2010.
—. *En ninguna parte*. Belgrano, 1981.
—. *Noche de revolucionarios*. Centro Editor de América Latina, 1972.
—. Personal conversation, May 19, 2011.
—. Personal interview, June 8, 1996.
—. *Puesta de sol*. Girol, 1997.
—. *Silver*. Atlántida, 1994.
—. *Un revólver para Mack*. Corregidor, 1974.
—. *Una epopeya de nuestros tiempos*. Catálogos, 2004.

Racial Re/Profiling: The Plays of Andrew Moodie

Abdillahi, Idil and Rinaldo Walcott. *BlackLIfe: Post-BLM and the Struggle for Freedom*. ARP Books, 2019.
Alexis, André. "Borrowed Blackness." *This Magazine*, vol. 28, no.8, May 1995, pp. 14-20.
Bailey, Pamella. "Toronto the Good at Factory Theatre: Moodie's New Play Tackles Racial Profiling and Gun Violence" http://www.suite101.com/content/review-toronto-the-good-a95162#ixzz1TdYHLxjv
Brand, Dionne. "Bathurst," in *Bread Out of Stone*. Coach House Press, 1994.
Clarke, George Elliott. "Must All Blackness Be American? Locating Canada in Borden's 'Tightrope Time,' or Nationalizing Gilroy's *The Black Atlantic*." *Odysseys Home: Mapping African Canadian Literature*. U of Toronto P, 2002.
Kershaw, Roger and Jim Langerfelt. "Oui, one of the most intelligent plays this season. Stage Door Reviews of Factory Theatre 1997-1998 Productions." 1998. http://www.stage-door.org/reviews/fact98.htm. Accessed July 30, 2019.
—. "The Real McCoy." http://en.wikipedia.org/wiki/The_real_McCoy
—."The Amazing Story of Solomon Moseby." http://historiclewiston.org/downloads/solomon_moseby.pdf
Mackey, Eva. *The House of Difference: Cultural Politics and National Identity in Canada*. U of Toronto P, 2002.

McKittrick, Katherine. *Demonic Grounds: Black women and the cartographies of struggle*. U of Minnesota P, 2006.
Moodie, Andrew. http://andrewmoodie.webs.com/apps/videos/videos/show/5976242-1-toronto-the-good-interview
—. "Too Canadian for Words/How Hollywood's sausage machine ground down award winning play" [Final Edition] *Toronto Star*, Mar 22, 1997: K8
—. *The Real McCoy*. Playwrights Canada Press, 2006.
—. *Toronto the Good*. Playwrights Canada Press, 2009.
—. *Riot*. Scirocco Drama, 1997.
—. *The Lady Smith*. Blizzard Press, 2000.
—. *A Common Man's Guide to Loving Women*. Scirocco Drama, 1999.
—. *Wilbur County Blues*. Mss. Courtesy of Andrew Moodie.
Moynagh, Maureen, editor. *African Canadian Theatre*. Playwrights Canada Press, 2005.
Sears, Djanet, editor. *Testifyin': Contemporary African-Canadian Drama*, vol. 2. Playwrights Canada Press, 2003.
Walcott, Rinaldo. "Dramatic Instabilities: Diasporic Aesthetics as a Question for and about Nation." *African Canadian Theatre*. Edited by Maureen Moynagh. Playwrights Canada Press, 2005, pp. 92-106
—. "Post OJ Black Men?" *Testifyin': Contemporary African-Canadian Drama*, vol. 2., edited by Djanet Sears. Playwrights Canada Press, 2003.

Dannabang Kuwabong's *Caribbean Blues & Love's Genealogy* and *Voices from Kibuli Country*

Goddard, Horace I. *Kola*, vol. 29. No.2, p. 37.
Hansen, Thorkild. *Islands of Slaves*. Translated by Kari Dako and Illustrated. by Birte Lund (Illustrator), Sub-Saharan Pub & Traders, 2003.
—. Coast of Slaves. Translated by Kari Dako. Sub-Sahara Publishers & Traders, 2002.
Gates, Jr, Henry Louis. *Wonders of the African World, The Slave Kingdoms Episode II*. Video PBS, 1999.
Goody, Jack. *The Myth of the Bagre*. Clarendon Press 1972.
Kankpeyeng, Benjamin W. "The Slave Trade in Northern Ghana: Landmarks, Legacies and Connections, Slavery & Abolition." *Journal Slavery & Abolition A Journal of Slave and Post-Slave Studies*, 2009, vol. 30, no.2, pp.209-221. DOI: 10.1080/01440390902818930
Kyoore, Paschal K. *Dagara Folk Tales*. U P of the South, 2012.
Kuwabong, Dannabang. *Voices from Kibuli Country*. TSAR/Mawenzi House Publishers, 2014.
—. *Caribbean Blues & Love's Genealogy*. TSAR/Mawenzi House Publishers, 2008.
—. *Naa Konga and Other Dagaaba Folktales*. Woeli Publishing Services, 1992.
Marsh, Clifton E. "A Socio-Historical Analysis of the Labor Revolt of 1878 in the Danish West Indies." *Phylon* (1960-), vol. 42, no. 4, 1981, pp. 335–345. JSTOR, www.jstor.org/stable/275012. Accessed 16 Apr. 2020.

Sebro, Louise. "The 1733 Slave Revolt on the Island of St. John: Continuity and Change from Africa to the Americas." *Scandinavian Colonialism and the Rise of Modernity: Small Time Agents in a Global Arena*. Edited by Magdalena Naum and Jonas M. Nordin, Springer, 2013, pp. 261-274. DOI: 10.1007/978-1-4614-6202-6_15.

The Holy Bible: *The New King James Version*. Edited by Arthur Farstad. Thomas Nelson Publishers, 1982.

Haunting the Human: M. NourbeSe Philip's Poetics of Un

Carr, Brenda. "To 'Heal the Word Wounded': Agency and the Materiality of Language and Form in M. Nourbese Philip's *She Tries Her Tongue, Her Silence Softly Breaks*." *Studies in Canadian Literature*, vol.19, no.1, 1994.

Demos, T. J. *Return to the Postcolony: Specters of Colonialism in Contemporary Art*. Sternberg Press, 2013.

Derrida, Jacques. *Spectres of Marx*. Translated by Peggy Kamuf. Routledge, 1994.

Gordon, Avery. *Ghostly Matters: Haunting and the Sociological Imagination*. U of Minnesota P, 2008.

Graham, Jorie. "Some Notes on Silence." *19 New American Poets of the Golden Gate*. Edited by Philip Dow. Harcourt Brace Jovanovich, 1984. 409–415.

hooks, bell. "Postmodern Blackness." *Yearning: Race, Gender, and Cultural Politics*. South End Press, 1990.

Jameson, Frederic. "Marx's Purloined Letter." *Ghostly Demarcations: A Symposium on Jacques Derrida's Specters of Marx*. Edited by Michael Sprinker. Verso, 1999.

Philip, M NourbeSe. *Book of Un with Undex*. Container, 2017.

—."Managing the Unmanageable." *Caribbean Women Writers: Essays from the First International Conference*. Edited by Selwyn R. Cudjoe. Calaloux, 1990, pp. 295-300.

—. "M. NourbeSe Philip / The Book of Un with Undex." *Container*. shop.acontainer.co/product/m-nourbese-philip-the-book-of-un-and-undex.

—. "Searching for Space: A Conversation with M. Nourbese Philip." Interview with Coomi S. Vevaina. *Open Letter* 9, 1997, p. 19.

—. *She Tries Her Tongue, Her Silence Softly Breaks*. Ragweed Press, 1989.

—. "We Can Never Tell the Entire Story of Slavery: In Conversation with M. NourbeSe Philip. Interview with Paul Watkins. *The Toronto Review of Books*. April 30, 2014. https://www.torontoreviewofbooks.com/2014/04/in-conversation-with-m-nourbese-philip/. July 10, 2019.

—. *Zong!* Wesleyan UP, 2008.

Quashie, Kevin Everod. *Black Women, Identity, and Cultural Theory: (Un)Becoming the Subject*. Rutgers UP, 2004.

Reed, Anthony. *Freedom Time: The Poetics and Politics of Black Experimental Writing*. Johns Hopkins UP, 2014.

Saleh-Hanna, Viviane. "Black Feminist Hauntology." *Champ Pénal* vol.12, 2015, pp. 3–28

Wynter, Sylvia. "Ethno or Socio Poetics." *Alcheringa*, vol. 2, no.2, 1976, pp. 78-94.

—. "Unsettling the Coloniality of Being/Power/Truth/Freedom: Towards the Human, after Man, Its Overrepresentation – An Argument." CR: *The New Centennial Review* vol.3, 2003, pp. 257–337.

Male Monstrosity or Failed Masculinity? Shani Mootoo's Literary Oeuvre

Cohen, Jeffrey Jerome. "Monster Culture (Seven Theses)." *Monster Theory: Reading Culture*, edited by Jeffrey Jerome Cohen, U of Minnesota P, 1996.

Espinet, Ramabai. *The Swinging Bridge*. Harper Collins, 2003.

Fanon, Frantz. *Black Skin, White Masks*. Grove Press, 1952.

Foucault, Michel. *Abnormal-Lectures at the College de France*. Verso, 2003.

Mohammed, Patricia. "Gender Relations." *The Encyclopedia of Caribbean Religions*, edited by Patrick Taylor and Frederick I. Case, vol. 1, U of Illinois P, 2013.

Mootoo, Shani. *Cereus Blooms at Night*. Grove Press, 1996.

—. *He Drown She in the Sea*. Grove Press, 2005.

—. *Moving Forward Sideways like a Crab*. Doubleday Canada, 2014.

—. *Out on Main Street and Other Stories*. Press Gang Publishers, 1993.

—. *Valmiki's Daughter*. House of Anansi P, 2008.

Natarajan, Nalini. *The Unsafe Sex: The Female Binary and Public Violence Against Women*. Oxford UP, 2016.

Persaud, Lakshmi. *Raise the Lanterns High*. Black Amber Books, 2004.

Reddock, Rhoda. "Freedom Denied: Indian Women and Indentureship in Trinidad and Tobago, 1845-1917." *Economic and Political Weekly*, vol. 20, no. 43, 1985, pp. 79–87. JSTOR, www.jstor.org/stable/40653663.

Tate, Shirley Anne and Ian Law. *Caribbean Racisms: Connections and Complexities in the Racialization of the Caribbean Region*, Palgrave Macmillan, 2015.

Postcolonial Ecologies and Sustainable Living: Reading Jenna Butler's Nonfiction

Clark, Timothy. *The Cambridge Introduction to Literature and the Environment*. Cambridge University Press, 2011.

Butler, Jenna. *A Profession of Hope: Farming on the Edge of the Grizzly Trail*. Wolsak and Wynn, 2015.

—. *Revery: A Year in Bees*. Wolsak and Wynn, 2020.

—. *Magnetic North: Sea Voyage to Svalbard*. University of Alberta Press, 2018.

—. "Contributor Spotlight: Jenna Butler." *Bellingham Review*, April 5, 2017. http://bhreview.org/2017/04/05/contributor-spotlight-jenna-butler/. Accessed 10 March, 2021.

DeLoughrey, Elizabeth and George B. Handley. "Introduction." *Postcolonial Ecologies: Literatures of the Environment*, edited by Elizabeth DeLoughrey and George B. Handley, Oxford University Press, 2011.

Garrard, Greg. *Ecocriticism*. Routledge, 2004.

Glotfelty, Cheryll. "Introduction: Literary Studies in an Age of Environmental Crisis." *The Ecocriticism Reader: Landmarks in Literary Ecology*, edited by Cheryll Glotfelty and Harold Fromm. University of Georgia Press, 1997.

hooks, bell. "Touching the Earth." *Moral Ground: Ethical Action for a Planet in Peril*, edited by Kathleen Dean Moore and Michael P Nelson. Trinity University Press, 2010.

Kerridge, Richard. "Introduction." *Writing the Environment*, edited by Richard Kerridge and Neil Sammells. Zed Books, 1998.

Huggan, Graham and Helen Tiffin. *Postcolonial Ecocriticism: Literature, Animals, Environment*. Routledge, 2010.

Ruekert, William. "Literature and Ecology: An Experiment in Ecocriticism." First published in Iowa Review, vol. 9, no. 1, winter 1978, pp. 71-86, reprinted in *The Ecocriticism Reader: Landmarks in Literary Ecology*, edited by Cheryll Glotfelty and Harold Fromm. University of Georgia Press, 1997.

Sayed, Asma. "Hope in a Time of Climate Change: In Conversation with Jenna Butler." Kwantlen Polytechnic University, October 29, 2020. Interview.

Sewall, Laura. "The Skills of Ecological Perception." *Ecopsychology: Restoring the Earth/Healing the Mind*, edited by Theodore Roszak, Mary E. Gomes and Allen D. Kanner, Counterpoint, 1995.

Soper, Ella and Nicholas Bradley, eds. *Greening the Maple: Canadian Ecocriticism in Context*. University of Calgary Press, 2013.

Witnesses from the Silentiaries: Claire Harris's Poetics of En(Dis)abling in *dipped in shadow*

Adams, Sylvia. "Three Poets Take Different Measure of Commitments to Reality" (*The Ottawa Citizen*, 1996, qtd. in "Voices from the Gaps," Driven to Discover, U of Minnesota, 2009. https://core.ac.uk/download/pdf/76348995.pdf

Clarke, George Elliotte. "Harris, Philip, Brand: Three Authors in Search of Literate Criticism." *Journal of Canadian Studies • Revue d'etudes canadiennes*, vol. 35, no. 1, 2000 Spring, pp.161-189.

Harris, Claire. *dipped in shadow*. Goose Lane Editions, 1996.

—. Interview with Nigel H Thomas. *Why We Write: Conversations with African Canadian Poets and Novelists*. TSAR/Mawenzi House, 2006, pp.115-130.

—. Interview. *West Coast Line*, vol. 31, no. 1[whole no. 22], Spring/Summer 1997, pp. 26-37.

— "I dream of a new naming."Interview with Janice Williamson. *Sounding Differences: Conversations with Seventeen Canadian Women Writers*, edited by Janice Williamson. U of Toronto P, 1993, pp. 115-130.

— "Why Do I Write?" *Grammar of Dissent Poetry and Prose by Claire Harris, Marlen e Nourbese Philip, Dionne Brand*, edited by Carol Morrell, Goose Lane Editions, 1994, pp. 25-96.

Hunter, Lynette. "After Modernism: Alternative Voices in the Writings of Dionne Brand, Claire Harris, and Marlene Philip." *The University of Toronto Quarterly*, vol. 62, no. 2, Winter 1992/93, pp. 256-281

Sheppard, Suzanne. "Claire fought injustice with pen, typewriter." *Trinidad and Tobago Guardian*, Sun Jul 01, 2018. https://www.guardian.co.tt/life/claire-fought-injustice-with-pen-typewriter-6.2.609515.28ea1cad72

The Catholic Study Bible. New Ameican Bible, Oxford UP, 1990,

Williams, Emily Allen. "An interview with Claire Harris." *Wasafiri*, vol. 16, no. 32, 2000, pp. 41-44, DOI: 10.1080/02690050008589709.

—. "Triadic Revelations of Exilic Identity: Claire Harris's *Fables from the Women's Quarters, dipped in shadow*, and *She*." *Beyond the Canebreaks: Caribbean Women Writers in Canada*, Africa World Express, Inc., 2008, pp.175-196.

Contributors

HORACE I GODDARD was born in Barbados and educated at Concordia University, McGill University, and the Université de Montreal. He has taught at Concordia and Laval Universities. A poet, novelist, and critic, his most recent works are *The Journey Home* (2010) and *One People: Two Worlds Apart* (2014).

HUGH HAZELTON is a Montreal writer and translator who specializes in the comparison of Canadian and Quebec literatures with those of Latin America. He has written four books of poetry, as well as *Latinocanadá: A Critical Study of Ten Latin American Writers of Canada* (2007), and translates from Spanish, French and Portuguese into English. He is a professor emeritus of Spanish at Concordia University in Montreal and former co-director of the Banff International Literary Translation Centre.

DANNABANG KUWABONG is professor of Caribbean and African Diaspora literatures at the University of Puerto Rico. His published books include *Caribbean Blues & Love's Genealogy*; *Voices from Kibuli Country*; *Myth Performance in African Diaspora Drama: Ritual Theatre and Dance*; *Mothers and Daughters*; *Rhetoric of Resistance, Labor of Love: The Ecopoetics of Nationhood in the Poetry and Prose of Lasana M Sekou* (Forthcoming 2021); and *Mothering, Community, and Friendship* (forthcoming 2022).

JUAN M SALOMÉ VILLARINI holds a bachelor's degree in Liberal Arts with a concentration in American Literature and Creative Writing from UMass Boston, and a master's degree in English as a Second Language from the Pontifical Catholic University of Puerto Rico, and has recently completed a doctorate in Caribbean Literature from the University of Puerto Rico in Rio Piedras. He currently teaches at the University of Puerto Rico in Ponce.

LESLIE SANDERS is University Professor in the Department of Humanities, York University, Toronto. She is the editor of the two volumes of the performance works of Langston Hughes and a general editor of the eighteen-volume *Collected Works of Langston Hughes* (University of Missouri Press). Her research and teaching is focused on Black Canada and she is webmaster of African Canadian Online (www.yorku.ca/aconline) and author of African American Autobiography, a resource for schools (www.yorku.ca/acc).

ASMA SAYED is the Canada Research Chair in South Asian Literary and Cultural Studies in the Department of English at Kwantlen Polytechnic University. Her interdisciplinary research focuses on Indian Ocean studies, postcolonial studies, and the South Asian diaspora in Canada. Her publications include five edited books and numerous articles in a range of periodicals, anthologies, and academic journals.

KATE SIKLOSI holds a PhD from York University. Her criticism has been featured in various journals and magazines including *Canadian Literature, MaComère, JAST*, and *The Puritan*. She has published four chapbooks of poetry, and her work has also been featured in various magazines and small press publications across North America, Europe, and the UK. She is the co-founding editor of Gap Riot Press, a feminist small press.